CW00518538

CLASSIC WHO
The Hinchcliffe Years

CLASSIC WHO

The Hinchcliffe Years
Seasons 12–14

by Adrian Rigelsford

BⓉXTREE

First published in Great Britain in 1995 by
Boxtree Limited
Broadwall House
21 Broadwall
London SE1 9PL

Cover design by Shoot That Tiger

Book design by Dan Newman

Colour origination by Jade Reprographics, Braintree, Essex.

Printed and bound in Portugal by Printer Portugesa Grafica LDA

A CIP catalogue entry for this book is available from the British Library

10 9 8 7 6 5 4 3 2 1

Contents

Acknowledgements

THIS BOOK would not have been possible, or even ever have happened, without the patience, willingness to dig into the past, understanding and co-operation of Philip Hinchcliffe, to whom I am indebted for agreeing to take part in this work. And, also, deep thanks are also due to the late Robert Holmes (RIP), who made time to talk all those years ago.

On the research side, immense thanks are due to Clive Banks, for digging deep in the vaults and coming up with the usual gems, and Dave Sheppard, for his continuing enthusiasm and dedicated archivism.

While at Marvel Comics, there was endless advice and support from the now sadly dethroned guiding forces behind *Doctor Who Magazine*: the inimitable Gary Russell, and the truly pukka Marcus Hearn, the true maestro of *Who* research. And latterly, there was tireless help from the new 'Guv, Gary Gillatt, my fellow Waits *aficionado*, Scott Gray, and their loyal Tom Baker-appreciating designer, Paul Vyse.

At Luke Books, as always, there are endless amounts of thanks to the guiding and understanding Gary Shoefield, Sharon Shoefield and Luke Shoefield, and also Paul Laurence and Paul Shoefield. While at Mastervision, thanks go to Steve Hodges, Gareth Watson and Sarah Brown. And, at Boxtree Books, immense appreciation goes to Jake Lingwood, for putting up with the madness, and 'The Guv', Adrian Sington.

In no particular order, the other usual suspects are the continually effusive Caroline Batten, Shaun Sutton, Barry Letts, David Maloney, Robert Banks Stewart, Michael E. Briant, Chris D'Oyly John, Graeme Harper, Andrew Skilleter, Rod Morgan, Rod & Krystyna Green, Kevin Davies, Kathy Dawn and her guitar, Mr Waits, Anthony Brown, Alan Adams, Richard Hollis, Steve Camden, Vicky Thomas, Glenn Mitchell, Derek Webster, Anthony Clark, *Dreamwatch*'s Gary Leigh, David Jackson, Janet Malone, Rob Lewis, Chris Fitzgerald, Ness Bishop & Brian Hudd, Ian Hogg, Simon Callow, Brian & Hildegard, Nicola & Mum and Midge . . .

Author's Introduction

SOMEBODY ONCE SAID that a story will never be completely told, unless you hear it from every viewpoint. If you were to try and tell the behind-the-scenes story of the making of any television programme or film production, for example, you would literally have to talk to everyone involved, right from the lead actors to the lowest ranking studio technicians. Everyone has a story to tell, and this book is basically the story from a producer and script editor's viewpoint.

Twenty-one years have now passed since Philip Hinchcliffe took over from Barry Letts as the producer of *Doctor Who*, and with Tom Baker as his leading man and Robert Holmes as his script editor, the production team took the series to new heights of popularity and controversy.

The actual production process, detailing exactly how the sixteen stories that were produced during this era were made, has been thoroughly documented in other books and magazines. So how could there possibly be anything left to say?

The premise of this volume is simple: Philip Hinchcliffe has pored over old production notes from his time on the series and rewatched all of his stories for the first time in almost twenty years. The resulting memories and observations that this process stirred up make up a large percentage of this book's text.

He has gone into the plans he had for the series when he first took over, he has detailed the failings and triumphs of certain stories, but mainly he has tried to recreate the thought processes and points of inspiration that led to the development of so many adventures that are now generally regarded as classics of their kind. But what of his script editor?

Robert Holmes worked alongside Hinchcliffe throughout his time on *Doctor Who*, and sadly he passed away in 1986. In 1985, during the research period for a book I was working on with David Banks called *Cybermen*, Holmes consented to give an interview about his involvement with the story, 'Revenge of the Cybermen'. As that afternoon progressed, the interview expanded and Holmes covered a wide range of memories from the time he worked with Hinchcliffe. This previously unpublished material fills in some areas that are not covered by Hinchcliffe's memories, and in some cases his words tell a different side to the story as his producer saw it.

Other interview extracts come from Barry Letts, who was questioned in November 1994, Shaun Sutton, who talked about his time as Head of Drama at the BBC in the late 1960s in August 1994, and David Maloney and Jon Pertwee, who were interviewed in July 1995.

This is not, by any means, the complete story. It is only an aspect of it. Call it an affectionate, partial memoir on Hinchcliffe's part, call it an over-extended interview. Whatever the case, *Classic Who – The Hinchcliffe Years* is a record of the time when *Doctor Who* was at its best.

Adrian Rigelsford
September 1995

Chapter One

The Next Regeneration

'In retrospect, I would have stayed on for another year . . . mainly to see what the new producer would have done with the series and my doctor.'

Jon Pertwee   **Interviewed July 1995**

NEARLY A DECADE had passed since William Hartnell had first made the character of Doctor Who a household name, and by the early 1970s the programme was firmly established as an integral part of the nation's staple diet of Saturday night television viewing. It was not so much of a cult as a part of our culture.

During the recording of the stories that would make up the tenth anniversary series, while Jon Pertwee was still at the height of his success as the third incarnation of the Doctor, some early signs began to appear that changes lay ahead for the series, both on and off screen.

Pertwee's producer, Barry Letts, had decided, along with his script editor, Terrance Dicks, to leave. After three years of working as the guiding force behind the show, they felt that it was time to move on to different projects.

'But we were persuaded to stay by Ronnie Marsh, who was the Head of Serials at the BBC,' explains Letts. 'He said, "I think that you're both fools to go. You've got a success on your hands, so capitalise on it! And, as far as I'm concerned, *I've* got a success on my hands as well, and I want to keep it going." Well, we said, "Oh, alright," and agreed to stay on for another year or so, waiting for the right moment to go.'

Such a moment presented itself within the next twelve months, when it became clear that Jon Pertwee would be leaving the series at the conclusion of his fifth year in the title role. There are varying accounts of exactly why he made the decision to go, the actor himself having gone on record offering a variety of reasons.

One was that he simply did not want to become typecast, and be forever associated with the role. Another told of how he had asked for a pay rise as an incentive to stay, only to find that his words fell on deaf ears. Shaun Sutton was Head of Drama at the BBC for this period, and offers the following as his own version of events: 'Jon Pertwee basically offered to stay on as Doctor Who, as long as there was the lucrative addition of a few extra numbers to his pay cheque. Well, I'm afraid to say, what with BBC budgets being BBC budgets, when it came down to the choice of having to pay someone extra to keep them on or paying the original wage to get someone entirely new, there really was no alternative other than to bid farewell to Pertwee's Doctor.'

By April 1973, Katy Manning was recording her final appearance as Jo Grant, the Doctor's companion for the past three seasons. Although the story in question, 'The Green Death', would bring the tenth season to a close as broadcast, the production team actually completed another serial before breaking up for their summer holiday.

Tom Baker as The Doctor and Elisabeth Sladen as Sarah Jane Smith on the set of the TARDIS control room, during rehearsals for PYRAMIDS OF MARS

Tom Baker during his first press call at the BBC's TV Centre in North London

Apart from acting as the opening adventure of Pertwee's final season, it also acted as an introductory story for the Time Lord's new assistant. However, there was a problem. A new character had been devised and an actress cast, but things just didn't work out as planned. The slate was wiped clean, and Letts and Dicks started again with a total rethink, and came up with the character of Sarah Jane Smith, an investigative journalist, as a replacement. Now Letts had to find someone to play her.

Ronnie Marsh was now leaving as the Head of Serials, and Bill Slater, who was the producer of *Z Cars*, had left that series to take over from him. One of the last episodes he had overseen of the long-running police series, which had started nearly eleven months earlier than *Doctor Who* in 1963, had featured a young actress called Elisabeth Sladen, who had greatly impressed Slater with her work, so he suggested her name to Barry Letts.

Following Slater's recommendation, Letts gave her an audition, and shortly afterwards she was offered the part of Sarah Jane. Her debut story was called 'The Time Warrior', which Robert Holmes had scripted, and it went before the cameras in May, with location filming being carried out around the grounds of Peckforton Castle in Cheshire. An instant rapport was established with Pertwee, and after the studio sequences had been finished the cast broke up for their summer holiday.

Letts and Dicks, however, chose to stay within the realms of science fiction, and moved over to BBC 2 to work on another show. From July until August they recorded six episodes of *Moonbase Three*, exploring the areas of science fact and probability which didn't really fit into the format they had established with *Doctor Who*.

Apart from editing these episodes, Dicks also had to contend with working on the incoming material for the rest of Season Eleven, and find a suitable candidate to take over from him at the same time. Both he and Letts needed replacements, as their departure was due to follow shortly after Pertwee's.

As the late Robert Holmes recalled when he was interviewed in 1985, he was more than a little suspicious of Dicks's ulterior motives, after he had been called in to see him under the pretence of 'having a chat about a few ideas and future projects': 'Terrance started being extraordinarily nice about some of my old scripts, so I knew that he was up to something. Before I ever got the chance to ask him, though, he went straight for the jugular and asked me if I'd like his job!'

Holmes accepted, finding the thought of such long-term financial security enticing, but he also relished the prospect of having the opportunity to restyle the show's format and, to quote, 'darken things up a little'. Luckily, when the new producer arrived Holmes found that he had much the same ideas as himself.

Holmes did have some experience of working as a script editor before. After serving in the Queen's Own Cameron Highlanders in Burma he had joined the police force, and then made his first move into the world of writing by becoming a journalist. After a while, he began to find that style of prose frustrating, feeling that he couldn't let his imagination run free. As a sideline, he began to write plotlines and samples of scripts for various popular television series from that time. In 1958 his first real break came with a commission to write four episodes of the hospital-based soap opera, *Emergency Ward Ten*.

'I began to get the odd nod of approval here and there, and even the occasional small cheque. *Emergency Ward Ten* gave me some sort of regular cash flow, which meant that I was able to take up writing full time.'

In September 1959, he took on the job as story editor on a thriller series called *Knight Errant*. One of the writers he brought in was Robert Banks Stewart, who had also made the move from journalism to television, and would later prove to be responsible for getting Holmes to write science fiction for the first time.

'Bob Banks Stewart had got a series up and running with ABC, who also made *The Avengers*, and it was basically this plot about aliens trying to corrupt society called *Undermind*. I did the last two episodes, and after that I began thinking about trying to write something along those lines.'

The result was a storyline for a four-part serial called *The Space Trap*, which Holmes sent in to the BBC, as they'd certainly made such things in the past, like the legendary *Quatermass* stories and a more recent venture called *The Monsters*. Unfortunately, it was rejected. This was in 1965.

'Shaun Sutton sent it back to me, with an explanation running along the lines of the fact that they'd stopped doing things like that. He did, however, open a line of communication with Donald Tosh, who was the *Doctor Who* script editor then, saying that he thought it ought to be redrafted and used on that programme instead.'

Holmes met with Tosh, and *The Space Trap* had the TARDIS and its crew inserted into the plotline, but nothing happened. Tosh never even acknowledged the fact that he had received it, and Holmes literally forgot about it, moving on to write for such series as *Intrigue* and *Mr Rose*.

In the spring of 1968 Holmes came across it again while he was in the process of moving house, and sent it to Peter Bryant to see if the *Doctor Who* team would reconsider it. This time

Tom Baker as Rasputin in NICHOLAS AND ALEXANDRA, which was made in 1971 and directed by Franklin Schaffner

THE SONTARAN EXPERIMENT: Elisabeth Sladen as Sarah Jane Smith, during the location recording at the end of September 1974

The Space Trap was not ignored. It was not long since Bryant had moved from being the programme's script editor to taking over as its producer. Past experiences had proved that scripts could fall through unexpectedly at the last minute, and he felt that it would be worth getting Holmes to develop his idea as a standby script, just in case . . .

In the middle of November, director David Maloney called an emergency meeting a few weeks before he was due to start recording material for a story called 'The Prison in Space'. The script, which was by Dick Sharples, was an out and out comedy and Maloney was certain that the finished episodes would prove to be a complete disaster. A replacement was needed.

Terrance Dicks, who had recently been promoted from being *Doctor Who*'s assistant script editor to full time script editor, stepped forward offering the recently completed drafts of the revised version of *The Space Trap*. He had spent the past couple of months working on the story with Holmes, guiding him as he reworked it, and Maloney quickly accepted it as a more viable proposition than the serial he already had.

So, after a title change to 'The Krotons', Holmes had his first *Doctor Who* story broadcast at the end of December that year, with the four episodes running on until mid-January 1969. It proved to be the first of five scripts he would complete for Dicks over the course of the next five years, prior to 'The Time Warrior' going into production.

Just before the annual Christmas break of 1973, Holmes joined the staff of the BBC and became part of *Doctor Who*'s production team. His first few days were spent observing the basic routine his new job entailed, as he trailed Dicks during the latter stages of studio recording on Season Eleven's third story, 'Death to the Daleks'.

Over the course of the next month or so, Letts secured the services of an actor to take over from Pertwee, and started to have various meetings with his successor as the show's producer. Both men came to the programme thanks to recommendations from Bill Slater. Letts had faced quite a task trying to find a new Doctor, as he explains: 'I'd been seeing all sorts of people, all "known" names and faces, but I hadn't been offering them the part. Just asking them whether they'd like to come in and talk about the possibility of being Doctor Who, with no obligation on either side.'

Jim Dale, Richard 'Mr Pastry' Hearne, Fulton Mackay – Letts was casting his net wide and considering all who came to see him. Some actors had their own reasons for not wanting to commit to the series. For example, there was Michael Bentine, the former Goon, who was keen to tackle the role, but lost all interest when it became clear that there would be no time for the kind of input into the scripts that he wanted.

Graham Crowden, now a familiar face from such programmes as *Waiting For God*, was intrigued by the notion of playing the Doctor, but just couldn't bring himself to offer to stay with the show for more than a year. Letts felt that the minimum period an actor should play the part was for three years, but Crowden couldn't face the prospect of having to turn down a good theatre role because he was stuck with the series for such a long period. Letts continues: 'In one of the everyday meetings I had with Bill Slater, he asked me how we were getting on. I explained that we hadn't found the right man yet, and he said, "Have you thought of Tom Baker?"'

Letts actually had no idea who he was talking about. While Slater was still working as a director, he had cast Baker as the Egyptian doctor in an adaptation of George Bernard Shaw's *The Millionairess*, which was screened as a Play of the Month on BBC 2. Baker was enthusiastic and wonderfully eccentric, and even then Slater thought that he'd make an ideal Doctor Who.

Slater arranged a meeting between Letts and the actor in the BBC Club bar. Nevertheless, Letts still had to see some of his recent work to be able to evaluate his potential, and as luck would have it Baker pointed out that his latest film was playing at a cinema in central London, and Letts and Dicks took the afternoon off to see the matinee of *The Golden Voyage of Sinbad*, featuring Baker as Prince Koura.

They were impressed. A phone call to the actor, who was earning a living as a labourer's assistant on a building site at the time, finally secured someone in the part, as Letts knew that he had found the right man for the job. Meanwhile, the new producer of *Doctor Who* was making the move over to the BBC from one of the regional ITV companies.

Philip Hinchcliffe's name had been put forward as a candidate for the job by Richard Wakeley, a literary agent with the Fraser and Dunlop partnership and an old friend of Bill Slater. After graduating from Cambridge with a degree in English Literature, Hinchcliffe had joined ATV in 1968, and spent his first few years there working in a variety of script related jobs.

He wrote scripts, worked as a story editor, ploughed through solicited and unsolicited submissions, developed ideas with writers and oversaw their eventual contracts, and represented ATV on the ITV Children's Network sub-committee. Hinchcliffe takes up the story.

'After I'd been doing that for a couple of years, I made the decision that the job I really wanted to do in television was to be a producer. In the end, ATV gave me a six-month stint as an associate producer, working on a now defunct daytime soap opera called *General Hospital*. Even so, my career still wasn't going anywhere fast enough for my liking.'

During the summer of 1973, Hinchcliffe took the unusual step of getting himself an agent to represent him as a producer. By and large, producers were permanently connected with television companies, so they didn't

THE SONTARAN EXPERIMENT: Ian Marter and Elisabeth Sladen, as Harry tries to free Sarah from one of Styre's experiments

actually need an agent, whereas actors, directors and writers, who were continually moving on from job to job, did.

Working through the network of contacts he had established with the London-based literary agents during his time as a story editor, Hinchcliffe went to Richard Wakeley, who agreed to take him on as a client. An interview with Bill Slater about the possibility of taking over *Doctor Who* soon followed, as Hinchcliffe explains:

'He seemed to be impressed with me. Not so much with what I'd done, but with my potential, so he offered me the job. He told me that the first thing I'd have to do was complete a drama called *The Girls of Slender Means*, based on a novel by Muriel Spark.'

This 'classic' serial had already been in preparation for quite some time. The scripts for each of the three sixty-minute episodes were ready, and a broadcast slot had been allocated for the project on BBC 2, but there was a problem. Because he was unable to secure the services of the director he wanted, the original producer had backed out of the production. Therefore Hinchcliffe's task was to take over and oversee the filming during the spring of 1974.

'Moira Armstrong was my director, which was a great help, as she was so experienced and I'd never actually produced before. The whole thing was a great personal challenge, as I had to get to know the mechanics of the BBC at the same time. It's a vast organisation, an immense bureaucracy with its own way of working. It was an entirely new professional and cultural experience, and I put a lot of energy into getting to know the system and how it worked.'

Shortly before location filming was due to begin, the entire production system at the BBC was crippled by a strike staged by the production managers. Filming schedules were in turmoil, and *The Girls of Slender Means* was postponed. The industrial action was not resolved until May, and by that time Hinchcliffe was too involved in preparing for *Doctor Who* to be able to return as the serial's producer. Martin Lisemore, who would go on to make *I Claudius*, took his place.

'The postponement actually helped me,' Hinchcliffe explains, 'because I had more time to concentrate entirely upon getting the first batch of *Doctor Who* scripts ready. I was trailing Barry Letts and getting to know Bob Holmes, while I decided exactly what I wanted to do with the series.'

With the arrival of Hinchcliffe and Holmes, a renaissance of the programme began which would see it reach new heights of popularity and controversy. As Holmes commented, '*Doctor Who* had a bullet-proof formula which could swing in whatever direction you pointed it. I don't think it would be unfair to accuse us of aiming towards a slightly "gothic" area. Tom always called it "Who-Noir".'

Philip Hinchcliffe pictured on location during a recording break, with one of his cast members

Chapter Two

Reconstructing the Myth

'If Tom's wild-eyed enthusiasm wasn't the first thing to hit you, then the sheer intelligence of the man was!'

Robert Holmes   **Interviewed March 1985**

Hinchcliffe was part of the generation who had grown up reading the *Eagle* comic, marvelling at the exploits of Dan Dare – Pilot of the Future, and his teen years were full of the classic cliffhanger radio serials of the 1950s, such as *Journey Into Space*, *The War of the Worlds* and *Dick Barton – Special Agent*, while on television, of course, there were the exploits to behold of a certain Professor Quatermass.

Authors whose work wholeheartedly embraced the fantasy field, such as H.G. Wells, Jules Verne and Aldous Huxley, whose futuristic visions in *A Brave New World* had stuck in Hinchcliffe's mind quite vividly, had all been read during his youth. Nevertheless, in the run up to taking over on *Doctor Who*, during the time that would have been spent on *The Girls of Slender Means*, he wanted to start afresh and take in as many different styles of storytelling within the genre as he could.

'I embarked on quite a wide reading plan, taking in a lot of authors I knew of or had heard about, such as Brian Aldiss, Isaac Asimov, Robert A. Heinlein and people like Frank Herbert. So,

'One of the first things I realised was that I had to understand the precise relationship that Doctor Who had with its audience. So I spent quite some time talking with Barry Letts and Terrance Dicks, basically absorbing the culture and the folklore of the series. In my opinion, Barry was a good and innovative producer. When I joined the programme, he was generous to me in the handover period, and gave me a thorough grounding in the mechanics of the show. Likewise, Terrance was invaluable in passing on 'the knowledge' of the Who tradition, and marking my card regarding writers, actors and directors. Something that struck me was the fact that I actually didn't know a great deal about science fiction.'   **Hinchcliffe**

having done that, I began to formulate a view of the programme as it was at the time, influenced to a certain degree by my early conversations with Bob Holmes.

'Without wishing to cast any criticism on previous regimes, it did seem that the series had become somewhat formulaic. If you wanted to be really critical, you might say that *Doctor Who* was getting into a bit of a rut.

'I sensed, but I didn't know how, that this freewheeling form could be reinvigorated, and that there might be a more imaginative way of handling the stories and the areas that you could take the Doctor into. I hadn't formulated that clearly, but it was one of the first hunches that I had over what we could do.'

The period from April to June 1974 was a time of change. It was the end of one era and the start of something entirely new.

ROBOT: Tom Baker on location at the BBC Engineering Centre at Wood Norton, Hereford and Worcester. This story marked the end of Barry Lett's tenure as the Producer of Doctor Who.

On April 3rd, Hinchcliffe and Holmes attended the first studio recording session of 'Planet of the Spiders'. Apart from still acting as the producer, Barry Letts was also in the director's chair for this adventure, having also had a certain degree of input into the script, working with writer Robert Sloman to develop what was basically a Buddhist parable.

The new producer and script editor were there to witness the regeneration scene that was being staged between the third and fourth Doctors, as Tom Baker made his first appearance before the cameras in the role, although he didn't actually have to do anything other than lie on the floor with his eyes closed.

Scenes involving the UNIT Headquarters and characters such as Brigadier Lethbridge-Stewart, elements that were such an integral part of the Pertwee era, were completed early on in the production schedule. This ensured that the actors were free to start rehearsals with Baker and director Christopher Barry on 'Robot', the opening tale of Season Twelve and the fourth Doctor's official debut.

Terrance Dicks had written the scripts for the story, after being commissioned by Robert Holmes as he took over Dicks's old job, and it was during the serial's pre-production period that Hinchcliffe became involved in making executive decisions on the show for the first time, as the look and the character of the new Doctor began to evolve.

'Tom wasn't really aware of the history of the programme, so he had to be filled in a bit and he proved to be incredibly enthusiastic, with a wonderfully infectious personality. I was very similar, in that I was full of ideas and drive as well, so there was a special kind of energy generated between us whenever we discussed the programme.'

During the period of research he carried out on the history of the programme, Hinchcliffe came across the famous quote attributed to Sydney Newman, one of the founding fathers of Doctor Who, when he was reported to have described Patrick Troughton's incarnation of the Time Lord as being a 'cosmic hobo'.

'It was a phrase that stuck in my mind. I liked the notion of the Doctor being a kind of wandering gypsy. He was totally unconventional, a rebel, somebody who was a bit different. "Bohemian" became the key word when we started talking to James Acheson about Tom's costume.'

Acheson was Robot's allocated costume designer, so the task of creating a look for the fourth Doctor that would not only stay throughout the rest of Season Twelve, but act as a template for whatever followed, fell on his shoulders.

Subconsciously or otherwise, one of the main influences was a famous pair of paintings by Toulouse Lautrec. 'Aristide Briant at Les Ambassadeurs' and 'Aristide Briant in his Cabaret' showed the renowned poet at the time of his readings in Paris during the early years of the twentieth century, wearing his uniform of a wide-brimmed floppy hat and a colourful flowing scarf trailing across his shoulders.

These two items of clothing became the main motifs of Baker's costume, which would survive throughout his seven-year tenure of the role. As Hinchcliffe explains, 'Tom was influential in all of this. Compared to Jon Pertwee's look, which I always saw as being a sort of Regency buck, he wanted to be a little looser and less of a man about town. Pertwee's style made him very much a Doctor of the 1960s – the ruffled shirts and the velvet jackets were the kind of thing you saw down the King's Road in London – but we were in the early 1970s. The *Zeitgeist* was slightly different, and I think that Tom belonged to that new era. His Doctor was an irreverent bohemian, and this was quite clearly articulated with his look. He could have walked straight out of one of the artist's cafés in Paris during the 1920s.'

The story behind the creation of Baker's scarf is now legendary within the BBC's Costume Department. Acheson gave a large amount of wool to a renowned knitter, by the name of Begonia Pope, with the simple instruction to knit a multi-coloured scarf.

The result was an item of some twenty feet in length, and it engulfed anyone who tried to wear it. Nobody had bothered to specify what the dimensions should be, so she just kept on knitting till the wool ran out. Baker adored it, relishing the opportunities it presented for using it as a prop, and after a few feet had been removed by Acheson the whole thing became more manageable.

Baker first wore it when location recording began on 'Robot' towards the end of April, with work overlapping on the last few days in studio for 'Planet of the Spiders'. A scene-shifters' strike caused chaos during production, but eventually Season Eleven's recording block came to an end when 'Robot' wrapped its studio material on June 7th.

Apart from Tom Baker, Ian Marter also made his formal debut as Harry Sullivan in this story. The character had been devised by Holmes and Terrance Dicks as a failsafe, just in case a younger man had been needed to

ROBOT: the story marked the debut of Ian Marter as Surgeon-Lieutenant Harry Sullivan, seen opposite with Tom Baker during the initial studio recording for the story in May 1974

21

THE SONTARAN EXPERIMENT: Ian Marter, minus the duffel coat worn throughout the story, during the six days spent recording in Devon

handle the action scenes if a much older actor had been cast as the Doctor. As it turned out, Marter ended up sharing that kind of sequence with Baker when it cropped up in the scripts.

While the cast broke up after this point for their summer break, Letts stayed on with the production team in an advisory capacity, as Hinchcliffe and Holmes started working on the task that lay ahead of them – namely, getting the scripts ready and the stories fully crewed up before the beginning of September, when they were due to start recording the rest of Season Twelve.

As Hinchcliffe explains, 'Unless you've actually written for television, or produced or script-edited a long-running series, you probably don't appreciate the sense of total dread when you look at the production dates ahead of you, and realise that there's no scripts and that you have to invent everything from scratch. Fortunately, I wasn't in that position, because Bob Holmes had already got a move on.'

While he was working with Terrance Dicks on structuring and commissioning material for Season Twelve, Holmes had followed a plan to, as he liked to put it, 'wheel out the old retainers'. By using familiar monsters from the programme's past, he felt sure that their presence would reassure viewers that it was still the same old series, in spite of the fact that there was a new leading man in the title role, but Hinchcliffe was not at all happy with this scheme.

'I was very keen to dump some of the stories outright, because the whole season felt a bit second hand to me, but, as Bob pointed out, we were just too far down the line to be able to even contemplate taking such action. So I decided to try and make something of the stories that we had.

'This was frustrating, because I'd made my mind up that I wanted to take the show into a more genuinely science fiction and science fantasy area, and generally broaden the appeal of the series so that it reached a far wider audience. We couldn't bring more children in, because I calculated that the ones who wanted to watch it were already doing just that. We had to make *Doctor Who* more adult.

'This could be done through the way that we treated the stories. I wanted to aim at a different level of realism, excitement and plausibility, and address different themes and styles of narrative. Thankfully, Bob was on my side.

'I was very grateful to have someone so senior in talent to work with. Bob belonged to a heavyweight generation of writers who've all but died out now. They learnt their craft with "live" television, and knew how to structure stories within the confines of a studio, and how to tell them with a limited number of characters. They were at ease using words instead of action.

'Bob knew how to construct plotlines and get exceptional material out of writers, but apart from anything else we got on extremely well, in spite of the fact that he was a lot older than me; I was 29, Bob must have been about 45. I think that he found my enthusiasm energising, and really saw an opportunity to slide a lot of his influence into the way that the programme was going . . . we became a really good creative team.'

Holmes was not the only one to comprehend what Hinchcliffe wanted to achieve and see the direction he

TERROR OF THE ZYGONS: Tom Baker as the Doctor, contemplating a piece of Zygon technology

Tom Baker at Wood Norton

wanted to take the show in. Tom Baker had also latched on to his producer's train of thought, as Hinchcliffe recalls.

'Structurally, there was a certain softness that seemed to have set in to the storytelling. When I thought back to *Dick Barton* and *Journey into Space*, I remembered sitting on the edge of my seat at the end of each instalment, and how frustrating the fact was that you had to wait a whole week for the cliffhanger to be resolved. To my mind, that kind of urgency and rigorous drive was missing from *Doctor Who*.

'So we increased the level of jeopardy that the Doctor and his companions were facing, and Tom got the message about what we were trying to do. He realised that it just wasn't enough to put the characters into a dangerous situation at certain points in each episode. He understood that through his performance, he could highlight the threat they were facing and convey a sense of heightened suspense and excitement.

'He got a firm grip on the fact that he wasn't only playing his character, but also that he was carrying the story. However you looked at it, Tom was the focal point, and he could articulate the rhythms of the narrative by the way he performed, and by the way he gave energy, stress and clarity to any given scene at any given moment.

'There was no doubt that he knew what we were trying to do, so we realised that we actually had a Doctor who could work for us in stretching the boundaries of where we could take the show, and that was great.

'When you saw Tom on screen, there was this wonderful, infectious grin, with these large magnetic eyes, and he also had a wonderful voice . . . although he gabbled his words at first, and we had to tell him to slow down and deliver his lines a bit more clearly. He also kept putting his hand in front of his mouth, it was an unconscious mannerism that I don't think he realised he was doing, but once you told him, he dropped it… But Tom's voice was very commanding, and in a way it became the Doctor's moral strength.'

He elaborates: 'Bob and I realised that we could really work on the Doctor's humour. There was a kind of earnestness about Jon Pertwee's Doctor, and about the programme itself at times, so we thought that we should turn Tom into someone who was in no way silly, but just full of surprises.

'A lot of people have said it, and it's perfectly true to say that any actor who's cast as Doctor Who has to be a one-off. He had to be somebody where the mould had been broken, so that you'd never come across another actor quite like him. Tom certainly fell into that category.' **Holmes**

'Some of the characteristics and qualities of the early Doctors were still there, like the fact that it was quite clear that he wasn't really human, that his brain was quicksilver and the fact that he didn't mind being rude… but, with Tom, he only did that to people who deserved it, and then they didn't even realise they'd been insulted. Such was the Doctor's charm.'

As September approached, twenty-two further episodes were due to go into production over the course of the next few months, in order to bring Season Twelve up to its full quota for a 26-week run on television. But things didn't go according to plan . . .

Chapter Three
Bohemian Rhapsodies

'Whenever you got a script through from Bob Holmes, there was always the game to play of guessing what horror film he'd worked into it!'

David Maloney   **Interviewed July 1995**

'**B**ASICALLY, the first two stories that I produced were planned as one production. In terms of logistics, it was staged as a six-part story. The ruse was simply that we would shoot 'The Sontaran Experiment' during the allocated location period, and then complete 'The Ark in Space' in its studio time. Bob Holmes had dreamt this scheme up, and it was all to do with his complete dislike of six-parters.'

During his last three seasons as producer, Barry Letts had established a routine of making two four-part stories and three six-part ones in each production block. Faced with having to work along those same guidelines, Holmes was keen to break it up as much as he could and get rid of at least one of the longer stories. Hinchcliffe explains the problem:

'There seemed to be a natural length for a *Doctor Who* story, and six episodes certainly seemed to push them beyond their limits. The narrative would either sag in the middle, or you'd have to come up with an elaborate subplot. That kind of story usually started to tread water by episode three and four, and the ratings always seemed to dip at that point as well.'

Holmes found that his strategy of making a two-part adventure alongside a four-part one appealed to his new producer: 'Philip got the bit between his teeth when I pointed out that nobody had tried to bend the rules quite like that before, so that's when he started to see it as a bit of a challenge. I put Rodney Bennett's name forward as the ideal director to do this, because I knew him from the past and had a hunch that he and Philip would get on.'

Hinchcliffe remembered: 'I went with Rodney on some of the location reccees, and he found this vast pile of rocks in the middle of Dartmoor which had a configuration that you could cheat with geographically. Bearing in mind the fact that we were using three lightweight outside broadcast cameras, it meant that their mobility would allow us to shoot and edit the story far more filmically. So, by setting up different angles, the same site could be used for a variety of story locations, such as the Sontarans' encampment.'

After ten days of rehearsals, the cast and crew made the journey down to Manaton in Devon, which was the nearest village to Hound Tor, the location Bennett had chosen in the middle of the moors. They arrived on September 25th, with recording due to start the following morning.

An outside broadcast van, known as a scanner, which had a scaled down version of a studio control gallery within, was parked about a quarter of a mile from the main shooting site. Hinchcliffe spent much of his time in the videotape engineer's van alongside it, where there was a monitor relaying the scenes as they were being staged.

THE SONTARAN EXPERIMENT: Kevin Lindsay as Field-Major Styre, returning as a Sontaran following on from his appearance in Season 11's THE TIME WARRIOR

THE ARK IN SPACE: Wendy Williams, Ian Marter and a kneeling Tom Baker, with the vast prop corpse of the Wirrn queen

'It rained nearly every day. I'd sit in there and watch what was being shot, pop my head into the scanner every so often and pass an opinion to Rodney, and then trek through the bracken to have a word with Tom and the actors.'

Everyone was staying at a pair of local inns, and the evenings were spent socialising in the bar rooms.

Letts actually spent some time on location with the crew, making himself available to help if any problems occurred, but Hinchcliffe seemed to be coping well. It was on September 29th when a near-disaster struck . . .

'Tom was going through the motions of a fight sequence with Terry Walsh. He was standing on this rock, which was very slippery because of all the rain, and suddenly he fell rather awkwardly. It was then that the message came through from Marion McDougall, our production assistant, saying that Tom was hurt.

'We got very friendly with all these local labourers and farmers, and took them on in a darts competition. Tom was part of the team. It was also my birthday during the shoot, and although I hadn't known the team for that long, they all gave me little presents. Roger Murray-Leach, our designer, was one of the principal architects of all this, and he gave me a tiny pair of child's booties, with a note attached which read, "Barry Letts' Shoes For Stepping Into".' **Hinchcliffe**

'She said, "It's bad. He can't be moved, this is an emergency, please contact the hospital." I thought, "Oh, my God! Here we are, four days into my first *Doctor Who* shoot, right at the beginning of the season, and my leading man's broken his bloody neck!"

'I raced down to the rocks, with thoughts flying through my head of having to recast the Doctor and junk the one and a half stories we'd done with him so far. The OB crew had some safety equipment, and they'd wrapped Tom in tin foil to keep him warm. He was incredibly pale and just couldn't move, so we all thought he'd done some pretty major damage.

'The ambulance eventually arrived, and they carted Tom off on a stretcher, so the rest of the afternoon was spent trying to complete any sequences where we didn't need him. That night was pretty sombre. We went back to the inn and I was waiting to hear the worst, half expecting a phone call to say that he'd be out of action for two or three months at least.

'Then suddenly, at about nine o'clock in the evening, Tom just came breezing into the bar, as large as life, with his arm in a sling. He'd damaged his collar bone, so we worked around him after that, using him in close-ups while Terry Walsh doubled for him in long-shots. After a couple of weeks, Tom was up and running again, just as though it had never even happened.'

One of the other problems the crew had to contend with involved the camera equipment, which reacted badly to the unrelenting damp weather. The cameras had to be kept functional.

'The cameraman used to take them back to the hotel at night, and leave them by the radiator to dry out. We got a rota system going, so that while two were out on site, one was always back at base drying out, so that it could be brought into play if one of the others started malfunctioning.'

Holmes had been unable to attend any of the recording days because of a problem that had occurred with the next story due to go into production, as he explains: 'I was going to write the Sontaran story, because I'd done "The Time Warrior" the year before, and there were one or two neat tricks that I'd dreamt up for their next story.'

Kevin Lindsay agreed to return and play a Sontaran for a second time, following on from his work in their debut story, but this was on the condition that the mask that he had to wear was made more lightweight for these new episodes. The actor had a heart condition, and during the studio recording of 'The Time Warrior', he had experienced extreme breathing difficulties inside the prosthetic and collapsed.

Hinchcliffe and Rodney Bennett ensured that suitable

THE SONTARAN EXPERIMENT: Ian Marter climbing down one of the rock faces found at Hound Tor, the location chosen by Director Rodney Bennet for the bulk of recording

THE SONTARAN EXPERIMENT: With Peter Walshe, Glynn Jones and Donald Douglas still in position, Stuart Fell steps in as a stunt double for Kevin Lindsay's Styre, as the lead-in to a fight sequence is prepared

29

THE SONTARAN
EXPERIMENT: Kevin Lindsey
as Styre waits out of shot,
while the camera is
focussed on Erak (Peter
Walshe) and Krans (Glynn
Jones) as they are forced to
torture Vural (Donald
Douglas) during recording
of one of the final scenes
of the story

modifications were undertaken, and the mask was reworked by its original sculptor, John Friedlander, who was also working on 'The Sontaran Experiment'.

Due to the pressure he was under to get the rest of Season Twelve's scripts finalised, Holmes had to relinquish the chance to write for his creations again. The opportunity to fine tune whatever Bob Baker and Dave Martin completed in his place, after giving them a highly detailed brief that even covered the creatures' methods of reproduction, never materialised, as Holmes explains: 'We had terrible problems with "The Ark in Space" in its original form. Terrance Dicks had suggested that we use John Lucarotti, because he'd done some good scripts for him on *Moonbase Three*, so we asked him whether he'd like to write for *Doctor Who* again.'

The idea of setting a story on a space station, where the surviving members of the human race were being cryogenically stored, had first been given to writer Christopher Langley. His resulting script, 'Space Station', was ultimately rejected, and the concept was passed on to Lucarotti, whose last scripts for the series had been broadcast during William Hartnell's era. But, Holmes recalls, it was not easy.

'John lived on a yacht off the coast of Corsica, so there was a real communications problem. A postal strike stretched his deadline to breaking point, and when the first couple of episodes literally thudded down on my desk, we could see that we had major problems . . .

'It was really overwritten, and had these elaborate special effects sequences, like this damn great hydroponic garden floating in space, and there was no way we could afford to do it. Philip went to Bill Slater and managed to get him to agree to let me do a total rewrite, which I finished while they were in Devon.'

'The Sontaran Experiment' finally came to an end, after six days of non-stop drizzle, on October 1st. Tom Baker's injury was such that he ended up wearing a neck brace to enable him to finish the shoot. He was due to be free of it midway through rehearsals on 'The Ark in Space', which began six days later.

Holmes had suggested a cost-saving measure that could be instigated with the sets for the story. He had devised a story plan for the season which involved the Doctor and his companions making two trips to the Nerva Beacon, the ark of the story's title.

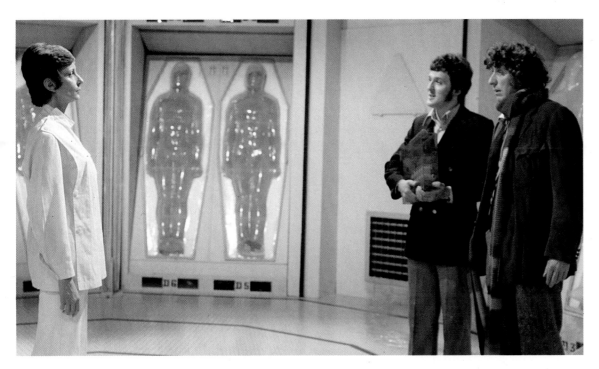

THE ARK IN SPACE: Wendy Williams as Vira, with Ian Marter and Tom Baker, rehearsing her initial scenes after her character has been revived from suspended animation

'We had "Revenge of the Cybermen" lined up for later on in the run, and Gerry Davis's original drafts had it set on a sort of space station, so I realised that with a bit of simple redressing, we could use "The Ark in Space" sets twice. Philip said it made "economic sense", which basically meant that he thought it was a good idea.'

Like Lucarotti's work, Davis would find that his story was the victim of a major redraft by Holmes by the time that it finally reached the screen. Although this caused a fair amount of resentment and anger from the writers who suffered this fate, Holmes saw it as being completely justified.

'In all fairness, the writers for that first year could have had no conceivable inkling of how Tom was going to play the part. Certainly with Gerry and John Lucarotti, it was a bit like reading scripts from the programme's black and white days, because those were the Doctors they'd written for in the past. I couldn't let past actors be used as a template for what Tom was going to do.

THE ARK IN SPACE: Kenton Moore during rehearsals on the set of the Nerva Beacon's solar stacks, with Production Assistant Marion McDougall relaying instructions to him from the Director, Rodney Bennett

THE ARK IN SPACE: Marter, Williams and Kenton Moore as Noah, rehearsing the scene where the Leader of the survivors of the human race is revived

'Those first two years of working with Philip had a heck of a lot of rewriting in them. This was purely because of the way we were trying to shape and hone down the style of the series, and introduce these radical changes in its presentation. I know that some of the writers took great offence to what was done, but the success of the programme had to be a priority in both Philip's mind and mine. So I'm afraid to say that it was inevitable that there would be casualties along the way.'

Roger Murray-Leach was due to handle the design for both 'The Ark in Space' and the Cyberman story, and discussions with Hinchcliffe followed, as he was keen to try and achieve something special with the look of both serials, as he explains: 'A lot of the story hinged around the unfolding mystery of what exactly this extraordinary environment was that the Doctor had landed in. There had to be a real sense of utter strangeness about this possible aspect of the future that we were seeing, so I talked a lot with Roger Murray-Leach about what he was going to do. He'd been working on light entertainment shows, and he was really looking for an opportunity to stretch his wings and show what he was capable of.

'Roger came up with a clever way of creating scale in the cryogenic storage chamber, by giving the whole set a sense of great height. And he used a mirror to create a false perspective effect for the camera, so that it looked as though there was an endless series of these honeycomb chambers. It worked really well on screen.'

As *Doctor Who*'s producer, Hinchcliffe's first official two-day recording block in studio ran from October 28th to the 29th, with episodes one and two of 'The Ark in Space' being completed in TC3, one of the BBC Television Centre Studios in North London. Before any of the actors arrived on set, the first thing that was

THE ARK IN SPACE: Tom Baker at one of the control consoles in the communications room, on Roger Murray-Leach's vast interlinking set

THE ARK IN SPACE: Sladen waits as Baker talks to the Assistant Floor Manager off-camera during rehearsals

actually done involved overlaying the story's title and its list of cast and crew members on the programme's opening and closing credits.

Bernard Lodge had created both sequences, using a technical process called slit-scan camerawork to create the effect of a multi-coloured tunnel of light on screen. Photographs of the TARDIS, Baker and the *Doctor Who* logo all moving towards the viewer were superimposed over this. A brief amount of time was always put aside to complete this on every story.

Hinchcliffe always liked to go down to the studios as early as possible, and be one of the first to see the sets fully erected. The impact of Murray-Leach's ark designs when you first saw them 'in the flesh' was extreme, as Hinchcliffe recalls:

'I remember going in through the studio doors and being just blown away. It was absolutely amazing. I mean, this thing was eighteen to twenty feet high, and people were coming in from other studios and programmes and staring at it in disbelief. For the first five minutes, it really was a thing of wonder. I don't think anything that big had ever been put up in the studios before.'

The alien creatures seen in the story, the Wirrn, were not actually deemed to be the greatest of design successes. According to Holmes, 'The idea was that these things were gigantic wasps, who stung a living creature and then laid their eggs inside it, so that the larvae could feed on the body as it mutated into another Wirrn. On paper that was fine, but I always felt that the finished product looked a bit like a knackered muppet, which proves how much I know, because they turned out to be one of the monsters that everybody remembered.'

Hinchcliffe adds his views: 'The bodies were a bit too shiny and new, they just didn't look organic enough. You had Noah being ravaged by this green virus, and the make-up department had a field-day with that, but the finished creature didn't quite have the right impact.

'I remember the scene being recorded where Noah fights the alien forces that are trying to take control of him, and there was this very powerful moment where he pleads with Vira to kill him. I remember thinking, "That's a bit strong!" and I was proved right, because when Bill Slater saw the finished show he said that we had to cut it.

'I was beginning to learn about the power of the actors, and realised that if you had energised, emotive performances, it really didn't matter how wordy the script was. As long as there was an underlying thread of plot that the audience could follow, you could actually achieve extraordinary results.

THE ARK IN SPACE: The upper torso and head of the dead Wirrn queen, top

Stuart Fell in one of the adult Wirrn costumes, on the set of the Nerva's rocket, above

'If we could write good character parts, with strong relationships and enough raw material for the actors to get their teeth into, we would achieve a level of reality that would give the show a very strong backbone. "The Ark in Space" proved that we could actually get away with some half-hearted visual effects because we weren't relying on the power of the drama to come from how monstrous the monsters looked, it was coming from the reaction of the actors instead.'

The second recording block on the story saw the production move to TC1, working from November 11th to the 12th. This was the last of the recording sessions that Barry Letts attended in his informal capacity as an adviser to Hinchcliffe, who was now proving to be more than capable of handling the demands of the series.

Story production on Season Twelve was now beginning to overlap. 'Robot' was finished and ready for transmission, and Rodney Bennett had started to assemble a rough cut of 'The Sontaran Experiment'. Location recces were underway in Somerset for 'Revenge of the Cybermen', with the story's assigned director, Michael E. Briant, searching for a suitable cave system to use which would meet with the script's requirements.

'Genesis of the Daleks' was undergoing final script revisions, with Holmes working alongside its director, David Maloney. The finale for the season had also been commissioned, after a six-part storyline by Robert Sloman called 'The Avenging Angel' had fallen through, with Holmes bringing an old friend in to write something to take its place.

Things had come full circle, and with an ironic reversal of roles it was now Holmes who had contracted Robert Banks Stewart to write a science fiction serial for him. Working from an idea he had developed, based on one of the legends of his native Scotland, Banks Stewart's working title said it all: 'Loch Ness'.

Hinchcliffe had managed to persuade one of the series' most prolific directors to return to work on this six-part tale after a five-year absence from the programme. With some 42 episodes to his credit so far, it would be the first of two stories Douglas Camfield would helm for the producer.

'There was never an eye of the storm,' says Holmes. 'It just kept going for six months, and then there would be this dreadful silence. That was the worst moment of all, because it made you realise that you had to start up all over again, with only one or two ideas left rattling around in your head, and an unending amount of blank paper that had to be filled in with scripts.'

Three days of night filming began from November 20th onwards, with Briant staging material for his Cyberman story in the Wookey Hole caves system. Because the site was open to the public during the day, potential delays caused by passing tourists could be avoided by working through the night.

Briant phoned in to Hinchcliffe every morning, as he had stayed in London to oversee post-production on

'It was always the same. When we got to about midway through a season, my office felt as though it had become part of some vast conveyor belt, with all these directors and writers passing through it.'
Hinchcliffe

THE ARK IN SPACE: Baker and Sladen on the main ark set during a recording break. Note one of the other actors is climbing out of his chamber

REVENGE OF THE CYBERMEN: Tom Baker on the studio mock-up of the Wookey Hole Caves, with Pat Gorman, in full Cyber-costume, looming up behind him

Bennett's two stories, and reassured him that the catalogue of accidents that took place did not involve a certain area of the caves. Hinchcliffe explains:

'There's always an insurance factor on any film or television programme, in case any of the actors are hurt or property is damaged, and there was this ancient stalagmite down Wookey Hole that was so many hundreds of thousands of years old, which was uninsurable.'

The stalagmite remained intact, but one of the cameramen fell off a rock and broke his leg, a make-up girl slid down an incline and gashed her legs badly and Elisabeth Sladen fell off a small powerboat called a Sizzla, and stuntman Terry Walsh had to dive into the underground river and save her from the undercurrents that were sweeping her away.

A stalagmite that had the same shape as a witch's hat apparently had a curse on it that would strike anybody who mocked it, so considering the camera crew dressed it up with a broom and a black cloak it would seem that the Curse of Wookey Hole took its revenge.

A certain degree of creative difference arose between Briant and Hinchcliffe back in London, the main one concerning the Vogans.

According to Hinchcliffe, 'The Cybermen seemed to have this autocratic, mechanistic way of thinking. Basically they were dangerous robots with delusions of invincibility, and that was part of their perennial appeal, but their actions were very unconvincing. They were fine while they were just marching around, and you could put music cues over them, but as soon as they stopped to speak they very quickly crossed the fine dividing line between *Doctor Who* monsters being realistic or implausible, and just became a bunch of actors saying their lines in rubber suits.

'The Vogans were a complete disaster. I just didn't like the way that the masks were sculpted, because the facial distortion was too extreme. Instead of being grotesque and creepy, they ended up looking like cartoon characters.'

It was quickly realised that the uniform physical appearance of the race would cause recognition problems for the audience, as you couldn't tell the difference between the main characters. This was resolved just prior to filming, as Briant gave instructions to the make-up department to add a variety of moustaches, eyebrows and side-burns to the masks to break up the visual monotony.

In his role as the series producer, Hinchcliffe normally made it a priority to have approval of such designs before they actually got to the manufacturing stage, but with the delays that had occurred finalising the script of 'The Ark in Space', which he had script edited as Holmes completed his redrafts, the Vogans had simply slipped through the net.

'The whole experience was frustrating, because I now knew what I wanted to do with the series, and here I was stuck with a story that essentially belonged to the old way of doing *Doctor Who*, despite all the good qualities that Michael brought as the director.

'I felt that the Vogans were playing their lines in what I call "Shakespearean projected shouting" mode. It just made them very clichéd.'

The story moved into TC1 at Television Centre for its first two-day recording block on December 2nd and 3rd. Holmes actually blamed himself for what he felt was a lacklustre script, as he explained:

'I tried to revamp the whole thing, and had no time to do an even passable job. Gerry Davis had produced a workman-like, commendable script, with roots so clearly set in the programme as he understood it from the 1960s, that Philip and I agreed that it would have been a huge retrograde step to shoot it as it was.

'Gerry did several redrafts, but it was still old fashioned *Who,*

REVENGE OF THE CYBERMEN: Kevin Stoney as Tyrum. Stoney's last Doctor Who work prior to this also saw him encounter the Cybermen, in the 1968 story THE INVASION

REVENGE OF THE CYBERMEN: A close-up of David Collings as Vorus. The masks for the Vogans were one of several elements Philip Hinchcliffe felt unhappy with on this story

so he threw in the towel and I took over. In retrospect, my big mistake was the Vogans, and I know Philip hated them … I take full responsibility, because they were my idea.'

Briant was unable to complete several key scenes during the location shooting, so the caverns Roger Murray-Leach designed for the studio recording to act as the main entrance hall to the Vogan Council Chambers suddenly became a makeshift battlefield. Hinchcliffe recalls:

'The Vogans ended up literally shooting at each other across ten feet of studio space.'

'There were some immense holes in the plot, like why were the Vogans bothering to try and shoot the Cybermen, when the simplest thing to do would be to run up to them and shove a lump of gold into their chest units? We just didn't have time to patch things up like that.' **Hinchcliffe**

Another difference of opinion arose between Hinchcliffe and Briant over the incidental music that was used as a score for the final episodes. The first time the producer heard it was when the finished episodes were screened for him for his approval.

'Michael had got this composer in called Carey Blyton, who was an extremely nice man, but his finished score unfortunately only added to the cartoon aspect of the Vogans. Now, post-production schedules were even tighter than the recording ones, so I took Carey into the Radiophonic Workshop, and told him that we had to make the music more exciting and suspenseful.

'So large chunks of the music in "Revenge of the Cybermen" were composed at an electronic organ, and made up to picture as it went along. I ran the picture and said, "Look, try something dramatic here," and Carey said, "What, like this?" played it, and it was laid down on to the programme's soundtrack without even being written down.'

'Revenge of the Cybermen' was completed with a second two-day studio recording block, with the cast and crew staying in TC1 and working from December 16th to 17th. 'We didn't manage to shape that story or revamp it into anything new, but we did succeed in giving "Genesis of the Daleks" a new slant. It came out with a different stamp and a different style to it,' Hinchcliffe reports.

Rehearsals were due to begin on the next story on January 2nd 1975, but Christmas hadn't happened yet, and Hinchcliffe and Maloney were working on a mini-script for a special event at the Blackpool illuminations on December 20th.

REVENGE OF THE CYBERMEN: Jeremy Wilkin as Kellman with Brian Grellis as Sheprah on the cave set built for the story, carefully designed to match the caverns of Wookey Hole, where location filming for the story had been shot

'Tom was asked to switch on the lights that year, even though he hadn't appeared yet, so David suggested that we ought to make something of it and take a couple of Daleks down there. So we concocted this sketch, which had Tom saving the mayor from the Daleks, and saving the illuminations from being exterminated.'

Hinchcliffe and Maloney travelled down with Baker and spent a couple of days staging the scene, which inevitably drew a vast crowd, even though Baker had yet to be seen on television. That event fell on December 28th, when the first episode of 'Robot' was transmitted.

Hinchcliffe relates the effect on the new Doctor: 'Tom said that his life changed after that first Saturday, because when he got on the tube train the following Monday people started to recognise him. That's the kind of impact that TV can have. He wasn't ready for the suddenness of celebrityhood, even though he knew it was coming. He got a hell of a charge out of that.'

'He just adored the fact that he was suddenly every child's best friend,' says Holmes, 'and that he was a "mate" of every man he passed in the street.'

Three days of location work was scheduled for 'Genesis of the Daleks', and Maloney found an ideal site to represent the desolate wastelands of the planet Skaro with Betchworth Quarry in Surrey, which he'd already used previously when he directed Season Ten's 'Planet of the Daleks'. Hinchcliffe has a telling story of the shoot.

'David was filming the opening scenes, and I arrived at the end of the day to see how things were going. All

'I always remember the week after "Robot" went out. Tom had an extra spring in his step, there was an extra spark to the twinkle in his eye, the grin was wider than ever. I was leaving the building with him, talking about the football results or something like that, and he was just being Tom … But when a child waved to him as we went out of the door, you saw the face change in an instant, and it wasn't him waving back, it was the Doctor.   **Holmes***

of the girls from the make-up and wardrobe department were grouped around the camera, standing about ten yards back. Their concentration was solely on the artistes.

'I was chatting to David, checking that everything was on schedule, and that he'd get all his shots done before the light faded, and suddenly I caught sight of these enormous rats. They were hopping around in the litter, directly behind the girls.

'I said to David, "Have you seen what I've seen?" and he said, "Yes, don't say a word. The girls will run off and we'll never get the shots in the can." So we kept going, half expecting a chorus of screams at any second, but they never noticed what was going on.'

A durable working relationship among Hinchcliffe, Holmes and Maloney was formed on this story, which

REVENGE OF THE CYBERMEN: Stoney waits for his cue as cameras are lined up behind him during studio rehearsals

GENESIS OF THE DALEKS: Tom Baker during the location filming carried out in Betchworth Quarry in Surrey, which doubled as the wastelands of Skaro

GENESIS OF THE DALEKS: Tom Baker watches as Marter rehearses reaction shots for the scene where Harry is scanned for concealed weapons

would see the director returning to helm three more stories for the team over the course of the next two years.

'David had a wonderful sense of humour,' recalls Hinchcliffe. 'He was very even-tempered, and very little phased him. After being an actor for a while he started out as a floor manager and went through the ropes until he eventually got to directing.

'He had a lot of input into the scripts for "Genesis", which had a sound basic story. The mechanics of the plotline were well worked out by Terry Nation, but some of the dialogue and characters, even for a *Doctor Who* script, were still a bit clichéd. So Bob Holmes got to work on patching that up.

'Right from the outset, I told David that I felt that the Daleks didn't represent that much of a threat, and he agreed, so he tried to give the production pace and energy. He gave it a more adult style, more panache.'

Holmes adds a detail: 'Terry Nation had set the opening scene where the Doctor confronts the Time Lord in a garden. It was meant to be this lush place full of gigantic orchids, and David would have none of it. He wanted Ingmar Bergman, he wanted *The Seventh Seal*. This was going to be Tom playing chess with Death on a beach, so we went for it.'

GENESIS OF THE DALEKS: Marter and Baker on the set of the Kaled bunker, with James Garbutt as Ronson, examining the contents taken from the Doctor's pockets

Studio rehearsals began on January 18th, with one of the largest casts from Hinchcliffe's entire era being put through their paces. A producer is largely absent from the rehearsal rooms for this period, and usually makes his first appearance at the 'producer's run', when the director and cast present a 'work-in-progress' performance of the script to garner any of the inevitable comments and input that will be made by him.

This was Hinchcliffe's first encounter with the characterisation that Michael Wisher had developed for Davros, the creator of the Daleks. Suffice to say, it was a rather different version to the one that appeared on screen.

'On that last day of rehearsal, the Daleks actors arrived for the first time, so they were being given an idea of where they had to position themselves, etcetera, for the scenes where Davros is showing off with this new creation of his. For rehearsal purposes, actors used chairs as Dalek bases. Now, Michael Wisher had been talking to John Friedlander about the mask he was going to wear, and John had warned him that he wouldn't be able to see a thing. So Michael had figured out a way to prepare himself for this experience…

'Anyway, the runthrough began, and David Maloney was at his most brisk, being very Sergeant-Majorish, shouting out directions, and suddenly he said, "Cue Davros", and in came Michael, squatting on his chair and hopping forward on it, wearing a brown paper bag on his head, barking out orders to the Daleks, who were

GENESIS OF THE DALEKS: Director David Moloney, to the far right, instructs a group of extras, demonstrating how they should attack Tom Baker, who is curled up on the floor in front of them

GENESIS OF THE DALEKS: Dennis Chinnery as Gharman, with Michael Wisher and Peter Miles in the background, waiting during a break in rehearsals

GENESIS OF THE DALEKS:
Rehearsals for Davros
(Michael Wisher) as he
unveils his latest creation –
a Dalek. Peter Miles as
Nyder is not in costume,
while Wisher is missing the
glove for his hand

hopping alongside him on their chairs.

'David gave me this subtle look and I could see his eyes twinkle, almost daring me to laugh, while all of the actors were taking it so seriously.

'Bob Holmes made a mad dash for the exit as soon as he saw Davros make his grand entrance. That only made matters worse, because I could hear him howling with laughter on the other side of the doors.'

The actual look of Wisher's mask stemmed from a meeting Hinchcliffe had with Friedlander when the producer suggested that he use the look of the Mekon, from the old Dan Dare comic strips, as a starting point for his design, by incorporating a high-domed shape to Davros's head.

The first studio recording block on 'Genesis of the Daleks' began on January 27th, with work being carried out in TC1 until January 28th. The second block moved the production crew to TC8, where two more days of work followed on February 10th and 11th.

'Whenever there was a scene between Davros and the Doctor,' Hinchcliffe reports, 'the script really came alive with a sparkling duel of minds that were on opposite sides, but apparently equal in certain ways. When we followed the Daleks wheeling around and shooting people, it became a typical run-down-the-corridor-and-zap-the-extras routine. The strengths of the story were in the performances, and Michael Wisher really created a worthy opponent for Tom.

'Overall, the scripts could still have done with some extra work. The cliffhangers had nowhere near the quality of surprise that I wanted to introduce, but we did our best in the time we had.

GENESIS OF THE DALEKS: Empty Dalek casings and Davros's chair left on the set during the dinner break

GENESIS OF THE DALEKS: Tom Baker practising with his yo-yo, which Hinchcliffe coached him to use – passing on the tricks he'd learned as a child

'When I first read the storyline, the allusions to the rise and fall of the Nazis were painfully obvious, and I thought we might have been able to subdue that element by going for a subtle design with the costumes. In the end, they all looked like SS officers, so the reverse happened, and they played up to the Nazi element quite blatantly. And also, as was typical with all six-part stories, it did sag in the middle.'

The final studio days ran from February 24th to the 25th, with work being carried out in TC6. When it came to staging a sequence where a Dalek gun was seen firing, the studio cameras had to be carefully lined up, so that the ray effect could be superimposed straight on to the master tape while the live recording was taking place. Hinchcliffe remembers the pressure.

'David had to finish the battle scenes between the Daleks and the Thaals, in the last five minutes we had of studio time on that last recording day. You could have cut the air with a knife.

'The atmosphere in a studio gallery was always very tense. You had to have a director who knew what they were doing, especially on a show like *Doctor Who*, or the whole thing could easily fall apart. There was always this mad rush, with a huge surge of adrenalin, to try and physically get the show "in the can" in the time that you'd been allocated.'

GENESIS OF THE DALEKS: Stephen Yardley as Sevrin, as the Mutos discover Sladen's body in the wastelands of Skaro

During the location filming of 'Genesis of the Daleks', which had begun on January 6th, it became clear that the season's final six-parter would not be completed in time for its scheduled broadcast slot. Hinchcliffe went to Bill Slater and explained the impossibility of the situation, and a compromise was reached.

Slater agreed to cut Season Twelve short, and bring it to an end after twenty weeks when 'Revenge of the Cybermen' finished, but he brought the broadcast dates for Season Thirteen forward, so that *Doctor Who* would return to the screens in the autumn of that year instead of January 1976.

According to Holmes, 'We were allowed to shift everything around, but it meant that we had to keep going and get on with filming the next bunch of stories immediately. We got ahead of ourselves in the schedules, but we had to agree to keep going and lose our summer break.'

Hinchcliffe and Holmes were keen to drop six-part stories entirely from the next season, and as a result Robert Banks Stewart's script was trimmed down to a four-parter, and the main cast were given a two-week break as the Dalek story was completed, before location was due to begin on what had been retitled 'The Secret of Loch Ness'.

After being refused the kind of budget he would need to film around the real Loch Ness, Camfield chose the village of Charlton in Sussex, and its surrounding woodlands, as a substitute. Four days of filming ran from March 17th to the 20th, with the crew moving to Littlehampton for sequences in a quarry and along a beach at Climping Sands, and the last day was spent working at Ambersham Common in Middlehurst. Hinchcliffe recalls the shoot.

'Literally, within the space of a few days, they had sunshine, rain, snow and hail. Douglas Camfield was tearing his hair out, and there was a huge amount of concern over how we could match the shots up. In the end, no one noticed…'

Reaction shots and background shots were staged on the common for the sequence where the Doctor is pursued by the Skarasen, which was the element of the scripts that had caused the director a great deal of concern.

'Dougie came in and said, "How on earth do you expect me to be able to film this?" Dougie was always attracted to scripts that had a military content in them as he had spent some time in the army. On this story he made sure that the actors moved and looked like soldiers.

His programmes were planned like a military campaign, but don't get the wrong idea about him. He was not autocratic, he was a man with a lot of humility, but he was a born leader and he was able to bring the best out in people.

'If he thought something wasn't possible, then he'd be into my office and say "I can't do this" or "If you want me to do this, you have to realise that the consequences will be this, this and

TERROR OF THE ZYGONS:
Tom Baker on location in
the village of Charlton,
near Bognor Regis. The
Doctor wears a bonnet for
the initial scenes of the
story, when he arrives in
Scotland with his
companions

TERROR OF THE ZYGONS:
During a break in studio
recording, Baker relaxes
while Sladen and Marter
chat with John Levene, as
RSM Benton, in the
background

*TERROR OF THE ZYGONS:
A close-up of the head of
the Skarasen model, with
the creature shown to be
the fabled Loch Ness
monster during the course
of the story*

this . . .". And that's what happened with the monster, because he couldn't see a convincing way of doing it.

'We talked about actually building a working prop. Today it's called animatronics. That was ruled out, and the special effects guys came in and, quite rightly, said that the only way to achieve a reasonable result was to use stop-motion animation. The problem was that we had set ourselves standards of what we wanted to achieve, and they had a standard of what they could achieve, and the two ways of thinking didn't match.

'Dougie storyboarded entire sequences involving the creature, and when the footage came back it looked ridiculous. Hardly any of the material that he needed could be shot, and half of what had been done was thrown out.

'In fairness, the whole scenario of using the Loch Ness Monster was too ambitious. The special effects guys couldn't do it properly in the time or with the money they had.'

The model shots of the Zygon spaceship worked far better, with the effect of the craft taking off out of Loch Ness actually being staged on location.

'It was a four-foot-wide model, which was pulled out of the water at the lake they were filming at. The same model was used for the sequences where the Duke of Forgill and the others are seen jumping out of the ship in the quarry. The model was placed in the foreground, and by using the right kind of lens Dougie made it look as though they'd jumped out of this enormous set.'

Only one partially finished Zygon costume was used during the filming, as James Acheson's design for the creatures was highly complex, and the body suits were taking time to make. Holmes takes up the story.

'James Acheson had this notion of giving them the shape of a foetus, and making them entirely unhuman. Both Philip and I had this plan that we really wanted to try and avoid using the 'men-in-rubber-suits' system for our later stories. That's why there was a lot of manipulation of the human form, through possession or mutation, because it gave a far more tangible reason for the threat to look like a normal man or woman.'

Hinchcliffe continues.

'When you normally designed a monster, you had a biped with an alien head and a human body, which worked against the overall illusion. I always tried to get to the heart of what the design concept would be that was underpinning the story, so that I could find out whether we could make the idea work, and then shape the rest of the material around what was possible.

'James said, "Oh, I know what we can do with these that's a bit different." The Zygons were half-reptilian/half-aquatic and their technology was very organic, so the way that he cracked it was to cut out the neck at the back of the costumes. This forced a certain kind of movement on the actors who were

*TERROR OF THE ZYGONS:
Keith Ashley as one of the
Zygons, and John
Woodnutt as Broton,
opposite. Hinchcliffe feels
that James Acheson's
design for the creatures
was one of the most
successful realisations of a
monster during his tenure*

wearing them, so that they had to adopt a certain posture and move accordingly. This made their entire level of mobility very alien, and it worked extremely well.'

After close to two weeks rehearsals, the production team moved back to TV Centre, with episode one and two of the story being recorded in TC3 from April 7th to the 8th.

This was the last appearance during Hinchcliffe's tenure as producer by Nicholas Courtney as Brigadier

TERROR OF THE ZYGONS: Technicians mingle with the actors on the set of the Zygon spaceship control room

Lethbridge-Stewart, a semi-regular character with the series since the late 1960s. It was also the penultimate appearance of UNIT during this era, because as with the Brigadier, Holmes and Hinchcliffe had agreed that it was time to phase these elements out.

'There were only so many ways for an alien threat to try and invade the earth and have UNIT defeat them,' says Holmes. 'The whole idea was becoming outmoded and very dated. It was totally out of sync with the kind of narrative style that we were driving the series towards.'

It was not a painless decision, as Hinchcliffe explains. 'Nicholas Courtney knew and understood the mechanics of the programme perfectly. He caught the flavour of it,

TERROR OF THE ZYGONS: Nicholas Courtney, in what would be his last appearance in the series until MAWDRYN UNDEAD, featuring Peter Davison's Doctor, in 1983

and knew how to send his character up in a very self-effacing way, and yet still play the straight bat at the same time.

'The basic decision to move away from UNIT was a strategic one, and had nothing at all to do with the quality of performance that the actors were giving. It's very difficult when you take over a show as its producer, because you realise that the livelihoods of the actors are affected by the decisions that you make. So when Nicholas, John Levene, who was Benton, and Ian Marter left, they lost the guaranteed income that *Doctor Who* offered. It's extremely hard, but that's the kind of life that an actor has to cope with.'

'I always liked Ian's portrayal of Harry. His character was this sort of amiable oaf, who had an inherently brave streak, so that although he didn't understand the danger of the alien threat he might have been facing, he was always ready to knock it for six if the Doctor gave him the nod. Personally, I think it was a mistake to get rid of him, but Philip was insistent.'
Holmes

Although both Levene and Marter would make brief return appearances during Season Thirteen, in 'The Android Invasion', this was effectively the last story for Harry Sullivan as one of the Doctor's travelling companions.

Hinchcliffe acknowledges that a mistake might have been made.

'In retrospect, I was wrong to get rid of Ian Marter. I can remember Bob saying, "Are you sure about this? He's a very useful character." I was adamant, and I overruled Bob on that one. He was very fond of the character, and he knew how to write lines for him with just the right balance of humour. It was nothing to do with Ian's abilities as an actor, far from it. I just wanted Harry Sullivan out of the series. I was very stubborn, because I wanted Tom and Elisabeth travelling on their own. With hindsight, I would have let Harry stay on until at least midway through the following season.'

Marter left after episodes three and four of the Zygon story were completed in TC4, working from April 22nd until the 23rd. This also marked the end of Season Twelve's production block, with work due to begin on Season Thirteen the next day.

TERROR OF THE ZYGONS: Marter, Sladen and Baker on the upper terrace of Stanbridge House, watching the Skarasen retrieve the homing device that's just been thrown in the River Thames

Hinchcliffe felt that Tom Baker's performance really hit the mark with 'Terror of the Zygons', which was the final title for the serial, changed shortly before it was due to be broadcast. Hinchcliffe explains.

'We dropped "The Secret of Loch Ness" as the title, because we didn't want to raise the audience's level of expectation. So we went for a very 1950s B-movie title instead.

'Tom Baker's performance was spot on in this story; crisp, with a terrific sense of dry humour, and a beautifully brisk, pacey delivery. He gave the whole thing a great sense of pace and urgency.'

From this point onwards, every story was now generated by commissions that Hinchcliffe and Holmes had made. All of the inherited material that Hinchcliffe had found frustrating and so binding had now been produced. He was now free to make the series as he had intended to all along, as Holmes recalls: 'Philip had a very specific view of what *Doctor Who* should be. It was after "Terror of the Zygons" when he started to bring his ideas to life . . .'

TERROR OF THE ZYGONS: Baker's Doctor trying to free the 'real' Duke of Forgill (John Woodnutt), the Caber (Robert Russell) and Sister Lamont (Lillias Walker) from the Zygon ship

TERROR OF THE ZYGONS: Baker on the set of the cell where the Doctor is held captive on the Zygon spaceship

Chapter Four

Looking through Cracks in Doors...

'Tom always entrusted us to make sure that we never went too far... Bob Holmes always said, "Add a bit of a healthy scare factor, but never try to terrify."'

Michael E. Briant   **Interviewed August 1986**

ORIGINALLY, Hinchcliffe and Holmes had structured the serials for Season Thirteen so that it would consist of six four-part stories and one two-parter, thus eradicating the six-part adventures that they felt so uncomfortable using.

Although some stories were generated through writers submitting their own ideas, the general routine that Holmes used was to feed them concepts which had been concocted with his producer, and wait and see what they came up with.

For example, Hinchcliffe wanted to do a story that put a twist on the idea behind Robert Louis Stevenson's novel *The Strange Case of Doctor Jekyll and Mister Hyde*, and have an actual planet go through progressive transformations, bringing its dark side to the surface.

Former script editor on the programme, Dennis Spooner, was commissioned to develop this into a plotline. His finished scripts, called 'The Nightmare Planet', were ultimately rejected, and the idea was passed on to Louis Marks, who started again from scratch and was successful, with his finished material seeing production as 'Planet of Evil'.

Other material that was under consideration included a storyline by Barry Letts called 'The Prisoner of Time', and one by Holmes's predecessor, Terrance Dicks, who was developing an idea called 'The Haunting'.

> 'There were specific themes that Philip and I were keen to cover. 75 per cent of the stories we did were always structured around basic guidelines that we laid down. It was never a case of telling the writers what to do, we just gave them the basics and a bit of a nudge here and there.'   **Holmes**

One of the areas that Holmes particularly wanted to build a story around involved Egyptian mythology, and the legends of the pharaohs. Lewis Griefer, an old friend of Hinchcliffe's, knew the subject well, so he was commissioned to work on the idea, as his friend recalls:

'I got to know Lewis while I was a story editor at ATV, and we used to talk over ideas for hours. I remember him telling me about how he worked on one of the episodes of *The Prisoner* ['The General', with Griefer using his frequent pen-name of Joshua Adam on the credits] and about how they ran out of money and they couldn't pay him. Patrick McGoohan gave him his Volvo instead of a fee.

'Anyway, the problem with Lewis was that he was incredibly complex with his plotting, which was fine for the other shows he worked on, like *Special Branch* and *Fraud Squad*, but you need a certain clarity with *Doctor Who* so that the audience can see where the story is going. Quite frankly, Lewis got lost in the script.'

PYRAMIDS OF MARS: Tom Baker, as the Doctor examines the sarcophagus in the study of the Old Priory, and realises it's far more than just an elaborate coffin

Griefer had to cope with terrible health problems as well, and a spell in hospital for an operation meant that his finished scripts were very late and Holmes had a lot of work to do.

'Lewis had scenes where Mummies were chasing people all over the British Museum, because it had something to do with alien seeds being stored in one of the relics, or a sarcophagus, and they were basically protecting them. The whole resolution was to do with the fact that these seeds would bring Mars back to life if they were planted in the soil on the planet's surface.

'It didn't really work, so I virtually rewrote the whole thing while we were doing the Dalek story, because Lewis had effectively retired to recuperate by that point. Philip had quite a lot of input into the scripts.'

Griefer emigrated to Tel Aviv to take up a job as an English teacher. During the gap in production after 'Genesis of the Daleks' had been completed, the producer joined forces with Holmes to finalise the initial drafts of the rewrite:

'We'd got the first three episodes mapped out, and couldn't quite see how to pull out the fireworks in the last one. Bob was very worried that the finale wouldn't add up to much, so we put our heads together and concocted all the trap sequences on Mars. I came up with the idea of using the two Mummy guards, where only one would answer a question truthfully, which came from a Kafka novel.'

This situation led to the Head of Drama Series making an extraordinary allowance for the *Doctor Who* production team. In normal circumstances, a script editor was never allowed to write his own material for the programme he was working on. Hinchcliffe was given permission to use Bob Holmes as the

PYRAMID OF MARS: Bernard Archard as Marcus Scarman, waiting to receive orders from his master, Sutekh

PYRAMID OF MARS: Baker, out of costume, and Sladen on the main study set during studio rehearsals

writer for up to two serials per season from that point onwards, so that the 'Pyramids of Mars' situation could be avoided in future.

Griefer took no on-screen credit on the finished serial, electing to use a pen-name, as Holmes had copyrighted the story to him and wanted to take no credit himself. Therefore, Stephen Harris appeared on the titles as the writer of each of the four episodes.

Whatever the case, both Hinchcliffe and Holmes were more than happy with the quality of the finished drafts they now had, as Hinchcliffe explains: '"Pyramids of Mars" contained the powerful notion that the Gods were actually space travellers. That meant that you could have the Doctor uncover an alien explanation lying behind a historical human truth, a very strong concept. You could take societies like the Incas or the mysteries of things like the Bermuda Triangle, and look at them through a different prism.'

PYRAMID OF MARS:
Sladen and Sheard try to
revive an unconscious
Baker, who has fallen
alongside Peter Mayock's
body

Paddy Russell had to find an elaborate country house, with nearby woodlands and a period-style cottage for 1911, when she started location recces as the prospective director of the serial in question. The property she found belonged to Mick Jagger, and permission was quickly granted for four days' filming around the grounds of Stargroves, near Newbury in Berkshire. It was perfect for Holmes.

'The house looked just like something in a Hammer film, which was just as well as we were practically ripping off every Mummy film they'd ever made. It was a preoccupation of mine to use famous horror and science fiction films as starting points for *Doctor Who* stories. It was quite clearly there for the audience to see if they bothered to look for it.

"Robot' was basically King Kong, 'Talons of Weng-Chiang' was The Phantom of the Opera, 'Planet of Evil' had bits of Forbidden Planet thrown in. The kind of people who spotted that were the ones that the joke was aimed at. The ones that didn't see through it didn't know, so nothing was really spoilt for them.' **Holmes**

Hinchcliffe has particular memories of Holmes's work here.

'One of Bob's favourite story devices cropped up in this serial, which was to explore the power of mental possession. He liked to show that a human can become a part of a far greater power, which could easily destroy them, and yet have this inner conflict raging, with their soul fighting against the inherent loss of their personality and humanity.

'That's why there's the scene where Marcus Scarman is seen fighting a losing battle when he confronts his brother, who seems to revive him for a brief moment, before he lapses back under the control of Sutekh and kills Laurence. It's a very emotive and shocking theme, which is why it's unsettling when you see the Doctor being used as a mindless puppet later on in the story.'

Studio work began on May 19th, with the main bulk of episodes one and two being staged in TC3 until May 20th. Some sequences were more violent than normal. Hinchcliffe comments:.

'The tradition of the programme was to show nothing more than ultra-safe violence, and I wanted to edge things beyond that threshold and present something more realistic.'

Baker's costume made the first of several changes, varying on the basic design that James Acheson had created, with a longer ruby-red coat being introduced. Hinchcliffe felt that it would enhance the heroic image of the Doctor, and make him a more 'dashing' figure. The motif of the scarf and hat, however, would always remain.

PYRAMID OF MARS: On location, filming around the grounds of Stargroves, which was owned by Mick Jagger at the time. Sladen takes aim, while Tom Baker stands behind her in full costume disguised as one of the robot mummies

PYRAMID OF MARS: Bernard Archard's Scarman confronts Doctor Warlock (Peter Copley)

PYRAMID OF MARS: The TARDIS lands in a store room full of Egyptian relics in the Old Priory, and the Doctor and Sarah realise it's the original building UNIT was built on, after the Priory burnt down in 1911

PYRAMID OF MARS: Gabriel Woolf as Sutekh, set free from his tomb at the conclusion of the final episode

The strengths of the story came from the style of writing that Holmes employed, as Hinchcliffe explains: 'Bob hit the nail right on the head with the dialogue. If you look carefully at the structure, it was not actually a technically demanding show when you compare it to something that involved futuristic sets, like "The Ark in Space" or "Planet of Evil". The fact that this was a period story gave it an extra quality and depth of texture, and I played to the strengths of the BBC which knows how to mount historical productions with panache and style.

'The story concept holds you all the way through. What technical effects there are work so well because they're married with such good acting and a convincing atmosphere. You get a sense of just how powerful Sutekh is through what he says. The character doesn't actually move until the last few moments of the final episode, and by that point you know that when this happens the Doctor's going to be in serious trouble.

'This showed a deepening quality of the imagination. The style that we wanted to imbue in the show was beginning to emerge ... Incidentally, Bob was very keen on Bernard Archard's character. I have this theory that people are attracted to actors who look like themselves, and Bernard had this large nose and strong Victorian chin, which is exactly what Bob had.'

PYRAMID OF MARS: Nick Burnell and Melvyn Bedford in full mummy costumes, rehearsing a scene with Scarman instructing them

Russell moved the production to TC6 on June 2nd, and the outstanding material that had to be completed for episodes three and four, along with a brief scene for episode one in the hallway of Sutekh's pyramid, was completed by June 3rd.

There was one difference of opinion, recalls Holmes: 'Philip was never happy about the alternative time theory I introduced, where the Doctor showed Sarah Jane and Laurence Scarman what the future would look like if he did not stop Sutekh. The reasoning behind this was simple: I didn't want the younger viewers to think that the Doctor's battles in the past were futile because the reality they knew in the present proved that everything would be alright. That whole scene underlined the fact that there was more than one timeline in the Doctor's universe, and therefore more than one possible aspect of the future.'

Hinchcliffe disagreed. 'The whole thing about showing the devastation Sutekh causes in the future was a very bogus science fiction cliché. It was dangerous because you didn't want the audience to think, "Hang on, that means in another timeline, Doctor Who gets killed." You had to emphasise the point that he couldn't be held by that strand of logic, because the very nature of time travel saved him from that trap.'

By now, Louis Marks had finished the final drafts of 'Planet of Evil' with Holmes, and David Maloney was preparing to start shooting film sequences at the BBC's Ealing film studios as the story's allotted director.

Hinchcliffe remembers the development of the story.

'Bob was beginning to try and bring his predilection and interest in gothic drama to the fore. There was no way that I would have countenanced doing that genre of melodramatic story in *Doctor Who*, but I was very keen to marry its influences and nuances of the style to strong science fiction concepts and premises.

'I started to convert the ideas that Bob was throwing at me with gothic touches through a kind of science fiction filter in my mind, and I suppose that 'Planet of Evil' was heavily influenced by these dark trains of thought that Bob was having.'

Holmes concurs: 'Louis Marks had done it in the script, but I really laid on the fact with a trowel that there were these guys in an ultra-modern, hi-tech space ship, and in spite of the fact that they had all of the most powerful weapons that their technology could throw at them, they just couldn't defeat this almost base, primitive power that was like some malevolent force of nature.'

The main setting for the story was to be an alien planet, which was part of the move that Hinchcliffe and Holmes were making to try and draw the series away from its traditional earth-based settings. Hinchcliffe explains:

'I went to see Roger Murray-Leach, and said, "How can we do a planet?" He told me it would be difficult, but he

could do me a convincing jungle instead. His main question was whether we could do it in a film studio. The advantage would be that you could change your angles with every set-up and create a greater sense of distance and space, and make it seem as though the set was far larger than it really was.

'By taking it away from the clinical glare of a television studio, and building it in an environment where a greater variety of lighting effects could be used, it would become a far more plausible image on screen. So, bearing this in mind, I agreed with Roger, and Louis and Bob drafted the final shooting scripts so that all of the planet surface scenes were set in a vast jungle.'

The complex vine-strewn sets were erected over a three-day period leading up to June 11th, when Maloney began shooting material for the story over another three days. The sequences involving the anti-matter creature were being prepared during this time. Hinchcliffe explains the idea.

'I had this image, a memory at the back of my mind, from a film I saw as a child called *Forbidden Planet*. The monster was a manifestation of the villain's id, and I was keen to go one step further and have the dark side of a whole planet appear as a psychological projection.

'The simplest method to do something like that seemed to be by using a spark-generator. The special effects team said that it wouldn't really work that way, because they wouldn't be able to produce a sufficiently clear outline and shape on screen.'

Maloney devised a system where a costume was actually made to represent the creature. After being filmed under extremely harsh lighting, the resulting image was then treated so that the reflected outline of the shape could be mixed with the picture being recorded on the jungle sets. The producer was reasonably pleased.

'The Colour Separation Overlay system they used worked quite well, but there's a lack of fluidity and movement with the creature whenever it appears. It just seems to loom menacingly. Apart from that, it was the kind of idea that I wanted to see. Although it wasn't that frightening to look at, the atmosphere it generated achieved a lot.

'The monstrous quality of the creature didn't so much come from actually seeing it, but it arose from the powerful effects it had. You saw the human-encrusted remains, drained of their life force. You heard the

PYRAMID OF MARS: Bernard Archard as Marcus Scarman on Mars, confronted by one of the logic traps set by the Osirans

PYRAMID OF MARS: Sladen and Baker rehearsing on the sets built to represent Mars, opposite, with the Doctor trying to reassure Sarah after she's been caught in one of the traps set by the Osirans

57

'Roger Murray-Leach came up with a design for the ship which was multi-levelled, so that whatever chamber you were in, be it the control desk or simply a corridor, there was always a different level for David to position the actors on, counteracting the normal sense of being studio bound. It meant that the spaceship really felt like a proper working craft from the future.' **Hinchcliffe**

rustling jungle and the trail of its approach. It all added up to something quite chilling, it was a case of less is more with that monster.'

Holmes was happy too.

'The creature was meant to be this force of untold anger, which could inflict unending damage whenever it crossed over into this reality, Philip was worried about the technobabble side of the script, but David Maloney managed to make it very clear that this thing was an immense threat.'

The first recording block on 'Planet of Evil', with the crew now working back at TV centre on episodes one and two, began in TC6 on June 30th, ending the next day on July 1st. The main sets for the Morestran spaceship were now used for the first time.

'Louis wanted the ship to be very sparse and uncluttered, so that there would be a vivid contrast to this wild jungle on the planet's surface,' explains Holmes. 'I tried to add little bits of stuff here and there that made the Morestrans sound like bureaucrats from the distant future. Their attitude was very much: if the monster can't physically be accounted for, it can't exist.'

Maloney insisted that the Morestran ray-guns were of a practical, rather than elaborate, design. When the actors pulled the triggers, the barrel of the weapons simply lit up briefly. Hinchcliffe continues.

'There was the occasional flash of light in the distance to indicate that something had been hit, but otherwise it saved on the time that would have been involved in lining up the shots to superimpose a ray-gun effect. With some of the battles, we would have been there all day.'

PLANET OF EVIL: close-up of Frederick Jaeger as Professor Sorenson, on the flight deck of the Morestran ship

PLANET OF EVIL: Baker's Doctor tries to reason with Vishinsky and Salamar on board the Morestran probe ship

'I was prioritising resources and effects, so that our money and energy weren't wasted on silly little tricks which would only be on screen for a second or so. Money was spent on creating atmosphere, and elaborate sets.'

Episodes three and four went before the cameras in TC3 on July 14th and July 15th. Holmes was keen for the resolution of the story to have the character of Professor Sorenson, as he falls into the anti-matter pit on the planet's surface, actually die.

'It was the natural through-line for the story to follow. The only way to placate the anti-matter monster should have been to sacrifice Sorenson's life to it, but Philip insisted that this was too harsh a finale, so we changed it shortly before the studio recording, and had the character suddenly appear at the edge of the pit, looking as though nothing had ever happened to him.'

PLANET OF EVIL: Michael Wisher as Morelli at the flight controls of the probe ship

According to Hinchcliffe, 'The story needed a final polish. But there just wasn't time for Bob to do his normal extra notch of tightening. I was always complaining about scripts being flabby and having a sense of dodgy logic, and he normally managed to patch things up. But at least the story was clearly sign-posted at every corner, so you knew what was at stake as you went through it.

'David was one of the directors who understood that the lead guest actors who were coming in for each story had to be of a certain calibre. They had to be able to convey the depth and inner conflict of the characters they were portraying, and be able to carry the weight of the story alongside Tom. Frederick Jaeger was a perfect example of this.

'It was actually David's suggestion that we cast a coloured actor as one of the crew members. I know that doesn't look at all odd today, but if you cast your mind back twenty years it was a much rarer thing to find a popular programme that was willing to take steps in that direction. He quite rightly said, "Look, if we're portraying a crew in the future, it really ought to be multi-racial."'

PLANET OF EVIL: Salamar (Prentis Hancock), Vishinsky (Ewan Solon) and Ponti (Louis Mahoney) examine the equipment in the geological base on Zeta Minor

The story submission that Barry Letts had made for the season, which had reached scripting stage, had not worked out and been rejected, and Terrance Dicks's effort had met a similar fate, but that was not the end of their continuing association with the series. While Dicks was given a brief to rework the basis of *Frankenstein* into a new story, Barry Letts took on the task of directing the next story to go into production after 'Planet of Evil'.

Holmes had asked Terry Nation to write for Season Thirteen while 'Genesis of the Daleks' was in pre-production at the very end of 1974. When the resulting script was finally ready at the start of June the following year, it had gone through a series of title changes. 'The Enemy Within' became 'Return to Sukkanan' and then 'The Kraals', before finally settling on 'The Android Invasion' just prior to the start of location filming.

By now, Hinchcliffe had gained a huge amount of confidence with what he was trying to achieve, and the general feedback was very positive. There was a buzz attached to the series, and people were now asking to work on it. Hinchcliffe explains his working method.

'It was a total, one hundred per cent collaboration with Bob Holmes, right from the planning of each season through to the structuring of the plots for every story. It was at the story stage that I could exert my influence on the texture and tone of the programme, and start to shape it in the direction I wanted it to go.

'Days were spent talking about stories, and I was often there for Bob's face-to-face meetings with the writers. I always tried to provide the central design elements which I knew we could achieve.'

Holmes tells his side.

'I always tried to put the writers at ease because I knew from my own experiences in the past that going to see a script editor could be a bit like going before a headmaster. These are the guys who will literally decide whether you've got a future with their series or not, so I always reassured them by saying that, come what may, they *would* write a *Doctor Who* story, and no matter how they felt at that precise moment, it would be a good one.'

Letts chose the village of East Hagbourne in Oxfordshire as his main location for 'The Android Invasion', which would allow him access to the Harwell Atomic Research Laboratories nearby, to double as the rocket centre, while Worsham Quarry and Bagley Woods fulfilled the rest of the story's exterior requirements.

'It was a story that we could shoot in a general UK location,' recalls Hinchcliffe, 'but like the setting of 'Pyramids of Mars' it used familiar sites and turned them into something sinister. The basic android concept at the story's core was very much a plot device of the 1960s. I felt like it belonged in *The Avengers* or *The Prisoner*, it had a rather old-fashioned quality to it.'

THE ANDROID INVASION: Tom Baker rehearsing an action scene on the set of the Tracking Station Control Room

Four days of filming ran from July 22nd to July 25th, and Letts remembers seeing Tom Baker in Bagley Woods, filling his hat with seeds from the wild flowers. When he asked what he was doing, Baker replied that he was going to plant them in the cracks of all the pavements around Notting Hill Gate, where he lived, so that when it rained the pavements would come alive with colourful blooms.

Hinchcliffe remembers the problems of this serial. 'It was always difficult to find directors who were up to tackling *Doctor Who*. Barry was at a bit of a loose end between projects, and what with him being an extremely experienced producer and director, I asked him to come and make one of the new stories for me. The reason why it's not entirely successful is because the result of this was two different styles of making *Doctor Who*, which didn't quite merge together.

'The android thread of the plot, with all its twists and turns building up into an evocative mystery, worked well. Then you came to the Kraals, and the perennial problem of how you make them, what they look like, how do you move and talk... and this aspect of the story was a huge failure in my terms. I think that Barry and his design team set out to make a *Doctor Who* as they understood the programme from his era. It was an uneasy combination of styles.'

According to Holmes, 'The Kraals were like thundering elephants, stamping around and bellowing all the time. The idea that these were exceptional cyber-surgeons was ridiculous if you stop and think about it. Philip was mortified when he saw what they looked like.'

Hinchcliffe explains, 'The Kraals were meant to be an immensely sophisticated and technologically advanced, gifted race, and yet they looked like a bunch of rhinos, with thick, hardened skin. That look and the idea that they were able to skilfully replicate humans simply didn't match. We never really cracked what they were going to look like beforehand.

THE ANDROID INVASION: A view of one of Philip Lindley's sets, showing the Kraal disorientation chamber

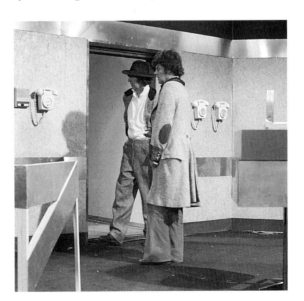

THE ANDROID INVASION: Tom Baker discusses a fight sequence with his stunt double, Terry Walsh, on the tracking station set during a break in rehearsals

THE ANDROID INVASION: Martin Friend as Styggron and Roy Skelton as Chedaki. Like the Vogans in REVENGE OF THE CYBERMEN, Hinchcliffe feels that the design of the Kraal masks didn't work well enough

'John Friedlander did an admirable job with the masks. Technically they hid the actors' face and still gave them a sense of jaw mobility, and the line around the back of the neck was concealed, so that shots could be taken from behind the creatures without any join showing … but when I saw them my heart sank.

'It was the Vogan situation all over again, with the actors booming away behind these masks with a mock-Shakespearean delivery.

'Part of the problem was the script. The action scenes were all constructed extremely well, and belonged to what was essentially Terry Nation's style of storytelling … but the scenes involving the Kraals had the most cliché-ridden dialogue, as all invasion of earth plots tend to throw up. I understand the problems Barry faced, because he had to have masks for the characters who then had to deliver yards of dialogue; not his fault.

'There was only so much that Bob and I could do, because we were becoming spread very thinly on the ground and there were only so many hours in the day. I couldn't be everywhere at every minute of the day as the programme's producer, and likewise Bob couldn't be expected to rewrite every single script that landed on his desk.'

Back in London, the first recording block began with episodes one and two going before the cameras in TC3 from August 11th to 12th. Ian Marter now made his final appearance in the series as Harry Sullivan.

'A lot of people were unhappy about the fact that UNIT was being retired from the series,' Hinchcliffe recalls. 'There was a part for the Brigadier, but Nicholas Courtney was unavailable, and it was rewritten for Patrick Newell [as Colonel Faraday]. So Nick felt as though he had just faded away from the series.

'Although there was no personal tension between the two of us, Ian Marter was upset because there were none of the scenes he was used to, where he was the third member of the Doctor's group.

'Harry was reduced to being a UNIT functionary, and even then he was playing an android version of himself for a large percentage of the story. Ian had a bit of an unhappy swansong. Things could have been handled a bit better than they were.'

The final two days of studio work saw Letts move his cast and crew into TC8, where the remainder of the material that was needed to finish episodes three and four of the story was staged over two days, running from August 25th to the 26th. During the rehearsal period for this recording block, Baker took a day off to record an appearance as the host of *Disney Time*.

Donning his costume from earlier in the season, he gave a series of introductions to clips from the vast canon of Disney films the programme could call upon, sitting in the stalls of an empty cinema. It was broadcast on August 30th, and led directly into the first episode of 'Terror of the Zygons', hence the return of the old costume to give the whole thing a sense of continuity.

With four complete stories now in the can, the series was sufficiently ahead of schedule to enable Hinchcliffe to give Baker and Sladen close to a month's break before they were needed to start work on the penultimate story of Season Thirteen.

It was at this point that Sladen told her producer that she felt it was time to move on, and agreed to stay until the end of the season and subsequently appear in the first couple of stories of Season Fourteen. The end of the thirteenth year was actually beginning to take on a different shape from how it had been originally planned.

Terrance Dicks had completed his work on 'The Brain of Morbius' and gone on holiday, after delivering the finished drafts to Holmes's office, and Robert Banks Stewart was midway through writing 'The Seeds of Doom', a six-parter which would bring the season to an end. Eric Pringle's storyline had now been dropped in favour of trying a new approach to structuring Banks Stewart's commission when 'The Angurth' had failed to work out. Holmes explains the concept.

'The idea with "The Seeds of Doom" was to try and do two separate stories, but keep the same narrative running right through it. The first two episodes would set the plot up and running, and at their conclusion, when the story had apparently been resolved, there would be a twist and a change of locations, with the story running on for another four parts.'

With Douglas Camfield signed up to direct that story, Hinchcliffe went to Graeme McDonald and asked for

THE ANDROID INVASION: Rehearsals on the set of the XK5 rocket, with Sladen, Ian Marter making a return and final appearance as Harry Sullivan, and Patrick Newell as Colonel Faraday

THE SEEDS OF DOOM: The opening scene – Charles Winlett (John Gleeson) and Derek Moberley (Michael McStay) excavate a Krynoid pod from the ice

more money for the budget of the season's finale, conscious of the fact that it would be a costly story to execute successfully.

Technically, the forthcoming extra cost would be partially compensated for by the fact that Dicks's *Frankenstein*-inspired four-part story, which saw Christopher Barry return to the series as the director for 'Morbius', would be entirely studio bound. There were no additional set pieces that required staging at the Ealing studio facility, or model shots that needed to be done at the Visual Effects Workshop; every aspect of the project was going to be mounted within the confines of TV Centre.

'Christopher Barry was a veteran *Who* director from way before I joined the programme,' says Hinchcliffe. 'He was a very precise man, who some people found a bit strong-willed, but underneath it all he was a very nice guy, and his results were usually very striking.

'I think the directors who had the technical know-how to cope with the series enjoyed it for the same reason that the actors did. It was an opportunity for them to let rip. The actors were given the chance to play larger-than-life characters, and bring their sense of humour to the fore, whilst the directors found that they could let their imaginations run wild.'

But before Barry was able to enter pre-production there was a major problem concerning the drafts that Dicks had delivered, as Hinchcliffe explains.

'It wasn't really pitched at the level we were aiming for, and the tone just didn't match our guidelines. The other problem was that it would have been very costly, because Terrance had this mongrel robot in it. Today it could be realised in a very sophisticated and convincing way, but with the resources we had then it would have been near-impossible to create anything that was anywhere near half-presentable.

THE BRAIN OF MORBIUS: Inside Solon's citadel, Baker and Sladen rehearse a sequence with Philip Madoc (out of shot). Colin Fay as Solon's servant, Condo, stands in the background

'So I gave Bob the signal to get on and completely rewrite it. I think he felt that it was his responsibility to some extent, in that it hadn't worked out after he'd given Terrance the premise to work with in the first place.'

Holmes takes up the story.

'Terrance was uncontactable. He was taking a break abroad, so there was no way to reach him and let him know that urgent rewrites were needed because the production schedule we were facing was extraordinarily tight. So I kept some of the elements that Terrance had dreamed up, but basically changed a lot of it around...

'The original had this robot using bits of bodies he'd retrieved from a mass crash-site of spaceships to build a new physical form for his master, who'd lost all but his head when his own vessel hit this barren wasteland. The problem was that his ego was such that when he's sewn on to this patchwork hybrid the robot had made he demands that a more suitable form is found for him, and that's when they began eyeing up the Doctor as a potential donor when the TARDIS arrived.'

Baker and Sladen returned to begin rehearsals on the story from September 20th onwards, with Barry starting to record studio material on October 6th and 7th in TC1. Hinchcliffe was not altogether happy.

'I thought that the concept would have been treated in a slightly more futuristic way, by both the script and the design team. What I hadn't bargained for was the way that they latched on to the whole Frankenstein

THE BRAIN OF MORBIUS: Baker and Sladen, with Philip Madoc as Solon, who cannot help but admire the shape of the Doctor's cranium...

THE BRAIN OF MORBIUS: Fay and Madoc between shots, waiting for the next sequence to begin recording

65

THE BRAIN OF MORBIUS:
Cynthia Grenville as
Maren, surrounded by
extras as the Sisterhood,
during a break in
rehearsals

element, and translated it on to the screen in such a literal and traditional way, with the body that Solon put together being very organic, and his laboratory being part of what was almost a castle. The atmosphere of the story turned out to be one of its strengths, but it also took the whole thing into an area that was gruesome and morbid.

'Once we got into the studio the whole thing began to evolve, with Philip Madoc giving a very compelling performance as the mad scientist, and Colin Fay was wonderful as his Igoresque sidekick, but the humour that was present in Bob's reworking of the script really wasn't enough to counterbalance the prevailing sense of darkness and morbidity. Apart from putting the brakes on in certain areas, the die had basically been cast, and I had to go with the flow of what was being done.'

But Holmes saw the story's strengths.

'I always thought that "The Brain of Morbius" was quite a unique *Doctor Who* story, because you couldn't categorise it in any of the normal brackets that the series had. It wasn't an invasion-of-Earth story, it wasn't an oppressed masses rise against their masters story, it wasn't a parable or parody … it was something entirely new. There had been the occasional alien who wanted to take over the Doctor's mind, but never one that wanted to go quite as far as Morbius did.'

Hinchcliffe agrees.

'We weren't settling for stories that just had a group of invading aliens in them, because we were always trying to take the series into new areas. "The Brain of Morbius" was a show that didn't resort to using the traditional story-telling techniques, and it really broke new ground in terms of presenting a different style of adventure.

'*Doctor Who* stories that passed through my hands were never pre-filtered or watered down for the audience. Admittedly, one of the consequences of taking that attitude can be that it makes the show a bit uneven, but it also gives it room for breath. Perhaps the producers that came before me and the ones that followed drew the line in certain areas, whereas I was always pushing forward and tried to turn any worrying elements into a story's main strengths. "Morbius" is a clear example of that point.

The second recording block on 'The Brain of Morbius' got underway in TC3 on October 20th, but technical problems meant that one of the major scenes remained uncompleted by the time that work finished the next day. Hinchcliffe managed to arrange a remount to stage the missing 90-second sequence. Fortunately, it didn't involve either Baker or Sladen, who were by now rehearsing for the next story.

Barry took Philip Madoc and Stuart Fell, wearing the full Morbius monster costume, into TC8 to finish the story off on October 24th. 'Stuart Fell,' says Hinchcliffe, 'was tied up inside that suit for hours at a time. He spent whole evenings recording in there and never made any real complaints, and it must have been hellishly claustrophobic. He was actually a very accomplished juggler, and whenever he was on set and not encumbered by the monster suit, you could always find him at the side of the set entertaining the crew with magic tricks.'

During a sequence in episode four a mind-battle takes place between the Doctor and Morbius, and several faces are seen projected on to a screen. The question has always been, were these the past incarnations of Morbius or the Doctor, since both of them were Time Lords? Hinchcliffe has the answer:

'We had pictures of Pertwee, Troughton, Hartnell and Tom, and the rest of the faces were the production team. Chris Barry rounded us up the day before recording was due to begin, put us in these period costumes and had tinted photographs taken of everyone. That's what was seen on the scanner.

'There was no subversion of the mythology of the series intended, but I just reasoned that it was entirely possible that William Hartnell may not have been the first Doctor Who. So yes, as far as Bob and I were concerned, the other faces were meant to be past Doctors. We did try and round up some well known actors

> 'There were certain quarters who always wanted Doctor Who to be the same show. They never wanted to see any signs of it evolving or progressing. They just wanted to see it as the same old kids' show that it had always been, with plenty of silly monsters to keep the young ones happy. I think you could safely say that Philip and I managed to ruffle a few feathers with that area of viewers and listeners.' **Holmes**

THE BRAIN OF MORBIUS:
Philip Hinchcliffe, in full
Cavalier regalia, as one of
the past incarnations seen
on screen during the mind
battle between the Doctor
and Morbius

who were working at the BBC at the time to do these cameos, but it didn't work out, and Equity went spare when they found out that we'd used production crew on screen.'

As commissions were handed out to write for Season Fourteen, the routine that Hinchcliffe and Holmes had established to plan out each year came into play once again.

'Bob and I would have a brainstorming session over the course of a couple of weeks, tossing in ideas that excited us both. These were gradually honed down and thrown to the writers to see what they could make of them. It was never a series where you could just sit in your office, call in a dozen or so writers and see what their ideas were; *Doctor Who* had to be driven by the imaginations of the producer and script editor.

'Plots were not the main element. Stories from our era that have stood the test of time had a very powerful premise or concept at their heart, which gave the narrative depth and layers. Really good stories always had an imaginative core, which gave rise to creating its own world. That's what we searched for: a script that brought its own unique universe with it, which then fed the imaginations of the director and the design team.'

Holmes puts it in similar terms: 'There was definitely an art to telling a good, strong *Doctor Who* story. It wasn't enough to have a writer say, "There's two planets, and they're at war with each other...". You had to give stories roots that ran deeper than the plot that you saw on screen. It had to be a part of some natural progression. Point A and C were already under way, and it's only with the intervention of the Doctor that point B is introduced, and all three areas are brought together by the time that you get to the story's conclusion.

'Some of the writers had a natural instinct to keep in tune with what Philip and I were trying to do, but there were the odd one or two who had other ideas, and thought that they could manipulate their scripts so that the programme went into an entirely different region. That's when I started to do a bit of rewriting.'

Faced with the task of finding a sumptuous country mansion and a location that could double for the wastelands of the Arctic, director Douglas Camfield had settled on Athelhampton House in Dorset for the former, while Dorking Quarry in the heart of Surrey was chosen for the latter, with the services of a snow machine being called into play to give the footage a suitably sub-zero quality in the finished serial. It was not an easy task, recalls Hinchcliffe.

'The Arctic expedition sequences started the story off well, so that it didn't seem as though we were about to put the Doctor in another quarry. One of the first questions I asked at the outset was, "Can we do a convincing take on the Arctic?" I went to Roger Murray-Leach and a new, up-and-coming visual effects guy called Richard Conway, and said, "We need a helicopter, we need a blizzard, we need a base camp which can be blown up – will it all be realistic?"

'Richard said that he could make these shots look really good if we staged them as a night sequence. Model filming always works well if it's done in the dark or in murky conditions, like the spaceship at the bottom of the loch in "Terror of the Zygons" had proved. Roger said that with fairly limited resources he'd be able to achieve a suitable snow-bound effect

THE SEEDS OF DOOM: Charles Winlett, fully mutated into a Krynoid, with John Gleeson donning an adapted Axon costume from the 1971 story, THE CLAWS OF AXOS

THE SEEDS OF DOOM: Baker and Sladen on location in Dorking Quarrey, in Surrey, which stood in for the Arctic

THE SEEDS OF DOOM: The Krynoid (John Gleeson) hiding in the generator shed near the Camp Five Arctic Research Station

in the quarry, and it went without saying that the interior of the base camp could be easily realised. These were the sort of points being raised well before production began.'

With Eric Pringle's script now cancelled, there was a brief period before Banks Stewart seriously started work on the first drafts of 'The Seeds of Doom', which was to be a four-parter. Hinchcliffe describes what happened.

'We lost the two-part story, which was something to do with a living rock that people made sacrificial offerings to, and so I went to see Bill Slater, and asked him whether we could cut the season down from 26 episodes to 24.

'He said an emphatic "No", because he'd committed the programme to a 26-week run in the schedules, so we simply told Bob Banks Stewart to make his story a six-parter. This was before he'd ever put pen to paper.. The story was planned out, structured and written as a six-part one right from its inception, as far as its author was concerned.

'The story reflects one of Bob Holmes's favourite themes, and it's one that he kept returning to. He had a theory that there's no such thing as good or evil in the universe; it's all just part of a process, and the side that you fall into simply depends on how you're made. He was fascinated by the notion of an organic life-form which lands on earth and causes havoc because it's neither intentionally bad or good, it's just that its "process" conflicts with ours and appears evil by comparison.

'So you have this inexorable life process, a system of rapid evolutionary progression that cannot be stopped: that's the point that the Doctor's continually trying to get across. It's an alien force of nature, and that gives the story its real power and, in a sense, its own morality.'

Five days of filming began on October 27th, with the first few days being spent in the grounds of the Dorset mansion. One of the sequences to be staged involved the Doctor being pursued by guard dogs, and the location sound supervisor, Vic Goodrich, wanted to record a separate sound track of the barking, which Camfield could later dub on to the finished serial. It was far from simple, as Hinchcliffe relates:

'The dogs wouldn't bark, so Vic, who had brought his own dog with him, brought it out to get the Alsatians barking. Unfortunately they started fighting. The dog handler, who was also playing one of the guards in the story, waded in to try and separate them, and his own dog bit him by mistake. Its teeth went straight through his leather boot, and there was blood going everywhere, so we had to rush him to hospital. Luckily it was not too serious; he came back the next day and was able to keep going through the rest of the shoot.'

Location filming came to an end on October 31st, and one of the last shots to be completed was actually staged back at Television Centre. The glass doorway outside the building's main reception area was used as the entrance to the World Ecology Bureau.

'Bob Banks Stewart's script was full of little, painterly touches here and there, all to do with character and atmosphere. Amelia Ducat, Harrison Chase, Scorby – all of these characters could have stepped straight out of a thriller or a crime story, which was Bob's forte. He loved writing eccentric parts, and really wanted to bring Amelia to the fore and give her far more to do, but we pulled back on that, and just kept her within her own part of the narrative,' relates Hinchcliffe.

'If you look at "Terror of the Zygons" and this story, there's a very humorous imagination at work. The Doctor becomes a bit of an action hero in this serial, and even runs around at one point with a gun in his hand, which was a great area of concern, but Bob Holmes put a line in about how he'd never use it and kept the integrity of the part intact.

Three studio recording blocks were scheduled for the story, with two designers sharing the job: Jeremy Bear handled the interior of the Arctic base, while all other aspects for the episodes were overseen by Murray-Leach. The first two studio days ran from November 17th to the 18th, with the cast and crew working in TC4. Hinchcliffe was pleased with the latest aliens.

'A great deal of characterisation through sound effects was involved with the Krynoids. Dougie had planned out the evolution of their mutative process quite carefully, working out the stages of how to take them from being a biped to what he called the "walking tent Krynoid".

'Dougie had found a new way to distort the actors' voices playing Zygons, which was very successful, and he came up with a kind of Krynoid death-rattle for this story. A bit of money was saved on the costumes because some of Barry Letts's old creatures [the Axons from 'The Claws of Axos'] were found in storage, so they were redressed and given a different paint scheme.

'There were very subtle touches. If you looked closely at the head of the biped Krynoid, there were clumps of hair around the scalp area, so that the last traces of the man this thing once was were still visible.'

THE SEEDS OF DOOM: Keith Ashley in the biped Krynoid costume, on location in the grounds of Athelhampton House in Dorset. Note the tufts of human hair on the creature's head, showing the last traces of the character that was infected by the second Krynoid pod, Arnold Keeler

THE SEEDS OF DOOM: The full Krynoid costume needed two people to operate it, with Keith Ashley and Ronald Gough inside. They had worked as monsters before for Director Douglas Camfield, playing Zygons in TERROR OF THE ZYGONS

By December 1st the second studio session was underway, with the production staying in TC4 until December 2nd.

'There was this inspired idea running through the last few episodes,' explains Hinchcliffe, 'that there was a revolution taking place, with the Earth's plant life turning against man so that the vegetation becomes the dominant life-form. It's a very dangerous area because you could easily slip into pastiche, and almost have a plant levelling a rifle at you, so this had to be something far more sinister and realistic.

'The Doctor is really the only one who understands the degree of threat that another life-force represents. He's the one who tries to understand the alien's internal logic and find a way to defeat it, while everyone else runs round panic-stricken. "The Seeds of Doom" was very much in the tradition of *Quatermass*, which Bob and I both had a sneaking admiration for. One man tries to deduce what the actual mechanics of the threat are, and in this case it's the Doctor.'

The final recording block of the story and the season ran from December 15th to the 16th in TC8. Holmes summarised the achievements thus far:

'Philip and I had done the standard *Doctor Who* yarns with our first season, we'd tried something new with the second and we really decided to pull out the stops for the third one. We wanted to see exactly how far we could stretch the programme's format . . .'

'The moral imperative is there throughout Tom's performance in this story. He's become a very authoritative Doctor, who doesn't suffer fools gladly. He conveys the priorities of the story, so that it's clear to the audience what's got to be done next. Although there are times when the situation is out of his control, you never lose sight of what he's trying to achieve, and neither does the viewer.' **Hinchcliffe**

THE SEEDS OF DOOM: Philip Hinchcliffe and Tom Baker at Athelhampton House, during the location shooting for the story

Chapter Five

The Galactic Renaissance Man

'Tom became far more than just another lead actor in a television series . . . I think he was pivotal in its success, because he believed in the stories . . . and more importantly, he had faith in what Philip and I were trying to do.'

Robert Holmes   **Interviewed March 1985**

'MY RELATIONSHIP with Tom was one where I'd keep him up to date with what was going on, and tell him about the ideas that were in the pipeline. Before we'd start a season, I'd say, "Look, Bob wants to do a story about this hand that crawls around," and Tom would go, "God, that'll frighten them!" and I'd say, "And I've got this notion about a vast mining machine full of robots which start to murder their human masters." If he could see me being enthusiastic about these ideas, then he'd get excited as well.

'It's no good keeping your central actor in the dark. We made Tom feel as though he was within the inner circle, part of the process that shaped and guided the programme. We'd talk Tom through the basic concepts so he'd have something to look forward to later on in the year, and both Bob and I really took him into our trust. Tom would come up with lots of ideas of his own, but he never interfered.

'Much the same kind of thing had to be done with the directors. You had to tell them in advance there was a story coming up that you really wanted them to do, and persuade and seduce them into doing it. *Doctor Who* was not a show that directors willingly took on. I went to Rodney Bennett and said that we were going to do a story in Renaissance Italy, and it was just the kind of script that he should come back and do, and luckily he agreed.'

The whole idea of opening Season Fourteen with a historical story filled Holmes with a sense of dread, because he could remember all too clearly why such ideas hadn't worked in the past:

'You had to have an immense sense of adventure to get them to work, and not just rely on the audience being impressed by the fact that the Doctor was talking to Marco Polo or Columbus. Philip saw the movie of Poe's *The Masque of the Red Death*, with Vincent as this nasty Renaissance duke, and he got this bug about doing the same kind of story in *Doctor Who*.'

Hinchcliffe was certainly enthusiastic about the idea: 'I was convinced that we could do a rip-roaring historical story, and that period of Italian history was full of wonderful elements that we could incorporate: religious cults, astrology, alchemy, etcetera. In a way, it had the same kind of formula as "Pyramids of Mars", because we used a period setting and had an alien power manifest itself through the

THE MASQUE OF MANDRAGORA: Baker during the confrontation with Captain Rossini's men during the first episode of the story

THE MASQUE OF MANDRAGORA: Recording the studio material, Baker rehearses with Sladen and Gareth Armstrong

THE MASQUE OF MANDRAGORA: Tom Baker wearing one of the elaborate masks used in the story

physical possession of a servile human.

'Bob Holmes was incredibly sceptical about the whole thing, and was convinced that there was no economical way to get any convincing location filming done.'

While he was a student in the mid-1960s, Hinchcliffe had once taken a group of American tourists on a tour of Britain, and one of the sites they visited was the village of Portmeirion in north Wales. This was basically an elaborate folly, designed by an architect who had been knighted, called Sir William Clough-Ellis.

'He had an irreverent attitude towards architecture,' explains Hinchcliffe, 'and brought a wonderful sense of fun to his work. He'd thrown all these different styles of buildings together, and imported hundreds of tropical plants to give the place a strange, unique atmosphere. I remembered my earlier visit and thought we might be able to achieve something if we filmed the story there. Although it wasn't strictly Italian, it certainly had Italianate features.

'I took Rodney Bennett there, and he

agreed that it was possible, so I made the strategic decision to go ahead as planned knowing the story could be shot with a certain degree of realism. Bob said that Louis Marks was the right man for the scripting because he had a very scholastic knowledge of the whole renaissance period.

'When his finished drafts came in they were in reasonably good shape, but the scenes involving Count Frederico needed tightening. I told Bob to beef the character up a bit, so he gave him a more colourful turn of phrase in places.'

An extensive period of location filming in and around Portmeirion ran from April 15th to the 20th, and Clough-Ellis actually visited the set while the crew were staging the Doctor's brush with death at the executioner's block, as Hinchcliffe remembers:

'He was a wonderfully alert, deeply eccentric character, who wore this ancient tweed suit, complete with Norfolk puttees, and had this mane of flowing silver-white hair. He seemed thrilled that there were all these soldiers running around his estate, looking as though they'd just stepped out of the past.'

Studio recording began back in London just under two weeks later, with Bennett overseeing a five-day recording block which ran from May 3rd to 7th in TC3. This story saw the start of a recording out of sequence, which Hinchcliffe had implemented.

'We started recording all the scenes located in one

THE MASQUE OF MANDRAGORA: Baker rehearses a sequence with several extras, as he tries to describe the missing Sarah Jane

THE MASQUE OF MANDRAGORA: Anthony Carrick as Captain Rossini on horseback talks to one of the extras playing a guard, while Baker talks to Director Rodney Bennett off camera

studio set at the same time, even if it only appeared in the first and last episodes of a story. Logistically, it made sense, because we didn't have to put the same set up twice, but it did confuse the actors who were used to working in story sequence, although they got used to it.'

A new TARDIS console room was now seen for the first time, featuring a wood-panelled design with an Edwardian flavour. Hinchcliffe explains his thinking.

'I was a bit irritated by elements that seemed to drag the programme back to what it was before, and the console room was certainly one of them. This was a time machine, and had to look like something that Jules Verne or H.G. Wells might have described. It had to be infinitely futuristic, but seem as though it had been built in the 1890s.'

'Philip wanted the console room to look as though it was something that Captain Nemo could have piloted. We wanted to explore, ever so slightly, the fact that the TARDIS was meant to be immense. Therefore there was no real reason to dismiss the idea that it might have more than one control room. I liked to think of it along the lines that there were four sides to the hull of the police box, so each one could easily be one of the exits from four different console rooms.' **Holmes**

Louis Marks's script underwent several title changes before its finished title was settled upon, varying from 'The Catacombs of Death' to 'Secret of the Labyrinth', and penultimately 'The Curse of Mandragora', before becoming 'The Masque of Mandragora'.

As pre-production began on the next story, Elisabeth Sladen was preparing to make her final appearance as a regular companion in the series, in what originally might have been an entirely different story. Hinchcliffe explains.

'When Douglas Camfield finished directing "The Seeds of Doom", he made it quite clear that he didn't want to do any more, but that he was actually interested in writing a script for the series instead. He had this notion about doing a 'Doctor Who Beau Geste' story, and was keen to use it as a dramatic finale for Sarah Jane.

THE MASQUE OF MANDRAGORA: Barry Newbery's radical redesign of the TARDIS console room, fulfilling Hinchcliffe's request to make it look like something from a Jules Verne story

'Bob Holmes was worried about whether this idea would work, and I had to fight quite hard within the department to be able to commission Dougie, but he'd given a lot to the programme and I felt that we ought to give him a chance. He had a deep fascination with the Foreign Legion's history, and really worked hard to make it an action-based story, which I would have seen through on the condition that he directed it as well.'

Camfield completed drafts for the first two episodes of a script he'd entitled 'Fortress of Darkness', with a battalion of troops trying to fend off an invasion force of aliens who had the chameleon-like ability to merge

THE HAND OF FEAR: Watson creeps up towards the entrance to the reactor chamber, as the Doctor and Sarah confront the newly regenerated Eldrad within

THE MASQUE OF MANDRAGORA: Norman Jones as Heironymous, court astrologer to Count Frederico, here seen in his guise as the leader of the Brotherhood of Demnos

into the surrounding sands. Sarah Jane would have been killed off in the closing scenes.

'The whole finale centred around the twist that the last of the aliens wasn't quite dead, and he shoots Sarah in the back. The Doctor then just sits cradling her in his arms as she dies, and the soldiers leave him alone, and we were meant to see him still sitting there in the middle of the night. When dawn comes the soldiers were going to get up and find a burning funeral pyre in the middle of the fort's yard, and just see the TARDIS slowly dematerialising alongside it.'

When this idea was eventually dropped, Holmes took his love of horror films as a starting point for a new adventure, which would use the image of *The Beast with Five Fingers* as its central core. To this end, he commissioned Bob Baker and Dave Martin to work on the serial, which went from being called 'The Hand of Time' to 'The Hand of Death', before finally settling on 'The Hand of Fear'.

'That idea didn't come from me at all,' Hinchcliffe explains. 'Bob generated that notion entirely. The problem with Baker and Martin was that you'd give them a story structure and they often tended to drift off in their own direction, although there was always plenty of energy and vitality in their scripts.

'The story was underplotted for the first half, with padded action scenes, and the way we overplayed the dangers of the power station was a bit of artistic licence on our part. The second half of the story, however, is totally missing the kind of qualities that were present earlier on. It's almost like an entirely different serial, and the Doctor is

THE HAND OF FEAR: Glyn Houston as Professor Watson with Frances Pidgeon as Miss Jackson in the background, on the studio set of the control room at the Nunton Complex

reduced to being a bit of a bystander … Bob Holmes was busy on other things, and really had to let this one pass through the net.'

This story marked the return to the programme of Lennie Mayne as a director, having last worked on the show during Jon Pertwee's final season, and sadly he was killed in a sailing accident in the Channel little under a year later.

'Lennie's death was particularly tragic,' says Hinchcliffe. 'His wife, who like Lennie was a former dancer, actually played Miss Jackson in the middle two episodes of the story, and was credited with her acting name as Frances Pidgeon. He was an incredibly popular guy – full of energy and fun – a real life enhancer who was always good to have around, and it was a terrible shock when he died. The same was true of Douglas Camfield; you see their work, and you remember the man.'

Six days of location filming began at the start of June, three days being spent around the grounds of the Oldbury Nuclear Power Station in Avon before moving on to the ARC Quarry in nearby Thornbury. One of the explosions that was staged resulted in severe damage to some BBC property, as Hinchcliffe relates.

'One of the cameras filming this avalanche of rocks was smacked by a chunk of stone which shattered the lens and knocked it for six. We used the film inside it, which didn't get damaged, and cut the film just before the cracks would have appeared on the screen as the glass broke. If the film had been exposed to the light nothing could have been saved.'

Work had begun on June 14th, and on June 19th Sladen's final scene in terms of the finished programme was shot in a secluded cul-de-sac near the quarry. Studio rehearsals began two days later, with the cast and crew back in London.

Her final scene with Baker, in the TARDIS console room as she bids the Doctor farewell, were staged during the last day of the first recording block, which ran from July 5th to the 7th in TC8.

THE HAND OF FEAR: Sarah Jane is pulled free from a rockfall caused by an explosion, while a concerned Doctor tries to assist. During the filming of the explosion, a BBC film camera was accidentally destroyed by flying rubble

THE MASQUE OF MANDRAGORA: Sladen and Baker share a joke during rehearsals in studio for what was to be her penultimate story as a regular companion

THE HAND OF FEAR: Judith Paris as Eldrad, waiting for her cue to move out of the dry ice during a studio rehearsal, below

'It was a botched ending,' Hinchcliffe recalls. 'Sarah is structured quite heavily into the story, and very much kept in the foreground, which was a concession to the fact that this was her last story, but we never really had a satisfactory last scene for her.

'Bob Holmes had a go, but I wasn't happy with the results, so then Tom and Elisabeth threw in a few ideas of their own, which I got Bob to try and adapt, but he couldn't get it to work and washed his hands of it. So we really had a goodbye scene that's heavily overwritten and lacks the crispness that Bob normally prided himself in ... although it does have a very human quality to it.'

The costume for Eldrad, which was used briefly on location in a partially finished state, was now used for the first time in its elaborate final form. Hinchcliffe remembered the difficulties.

'We had to allocate a lot of extra time to get Judith Paris ready, particularly where the intricate facial appliances were concerned. This was a problem we avoided with Stephen Thorne when he arrived to play the male Eldrad because the design was simplified so that the hood of his costume fitted around his face. By keeping the lighting down on him, it didn't seem as rough-edged on screen as it actually was.'

Two final days were spent recording on the story, again in TC8, from July 19th to the 20th. While the production team were in studio for this story, the hand of the title caused problems that were not that easy to solve, as Hinchcliffe explains.

'That final scene should have been so much better, but we hit a mental brick wall. How could we sum up the kind of bond that had built up between Sarah and the Doctor successfully, and keep the pair of them in character? It just didn't play at all well.'   **Holmes**

THE HAND OF FEAR: Baker poses with the prop hand built for they story

'There were various versions of it, ranging from a plaster one to a rubber one that was hollow, and could be worn by an operator and moved. During the dinner break on one of the last days, someone crept into the studio and stole the hand! We had to line up the shots that evening, so you couldn't see that a much poorer version was being used instead.'

The lead actors themselves were never a problem though, often taking an active role in the creative process.

'Elisabeth was an extremely accomplished actress, and was totally in tune with the styles and intentions of the show. She was good at pointing up the narrative of the story, as was Tom, and brought a sense of reality to her performances …

'Tom came to see Bob and I and said, "Now that Liz has gone, do I really need another companion?" I sat him down and explained how we needed one to split the plots off into different routes, and that he also needed someone to talk to. Tom said, "Can't I talk to myself?" I pointed out that it would become pretty boring for an audience after a while.'

Hinchcliffe agreed to do one story with the Doctor on a solo adventure. The plotline came from his penchant for stories where a character's actions in the past bring a very real jeopardy to the present, which they then have to contend with.

'In my mind's eye, it would be the equivalent of a CIA conspiracy-theory thriller, with echoes of the Kennedy assassination. The Doctor would be framed and have to prove his innocence, and in doing so expose the real villains of the piece. Bob said that the most obvious society to place this in would be the Time Lords.'

Holmes's next logical step in developing the storyline was to introduce the only real opponent who could pose a threat to the Doctor within that context – the Master.

THE HAND OF FEAR: Tom Baker and Elisabeth Sladen on location in the ARC Quarrey in Avon

'A few years had passed since Roger Delgado had died, so we agreed that enough time had passed to bring the character back, and I got the idea that the Master's whole *raison d'être* was to get a fresh lifeline from his home planet. That was fine, but the real dilemma was over how to present the Time Lords.

'I think that there were several instances in other shows when villains, monsters, or whatever, had made it clear that even though these guys were all-powerful, they were deeply flawed. If they had a strict policy of non-intervention, why did they choose to manipulate the Doctor and send him on so many missions? There was a deep hypocrisy at work, and that's where the notion came from of making them rather effete in general, with a dirty tricks brigade lurking underneath … just like any government.'

Holmes's draft of 'The Dangerous Assassin' became 'The Deadly Assassin', and David Maloney returned to the series to direct this story, which required five days of location filming to realise the bizarre mind-battle sequence that Holmes had planned between the Doctor and the Master's co-conspirator, Chancellor Goth.

'I wanted to see how far we could go. This was all devised as a battle of wits and imagination, with Goth coming up with more and more twisted ways to try and kill the Doctor. I tried to put as many subtle references in there to my favourite movies as I could: the Samurai from Kurosawa's *The Seven Samurai*, the plane chase from *North By Northwest*, the hero trapped on the rails with an oncoming train speeding towards him from the Saturday morning serials of my youth.'

THE DEADLY ASSASSIN: Brian Nolan as the Camera Technician, above, about to meet his fate at the hands of the Master. The vast set for the Panopticon, below, with extras as Time Lords and Chancellery Guards

After last using the site for 'Genesis of the Daleks', Maloney started filming at Betchworth Quarry in Surrey on July 26th for three days. The extensive, almost tropical gardens at the Royal Alexandra and Albert School near Merstham, again in Surrey, were the next venue for shooting from July 29th to 30th, with the final afternoon being spent at Redhill aerodrome, where model sequences were shot with a remote controlled one-third scale biplane, with low angled camerawork giving it a very authentic look in the finished programme.

'Philip was very supportive of what I was trying to do,' says Holmes, 'and although I think he was initially a bit concerned about whether David Maloney would get the point of what I was aiming for, as soon as David said how enthusiastic he was about doing it, Philip began to get excited as well.'

Working alongside Maloney for the second of their *Doctor Who* serials together was designer Roger Murray-Leach, and the

THE DEADLY ASSASSIN: Baker during studio rehearsals, above, being led into the Panopticon. Production Assistant Nicholas Howard John can be seen to the far right; Baker in full Time Lord ceremonial robes during a break, below

backbone of the team who would visually realise the story was completed with the return of James Acheson as costume designer. Acheson felt that the budget he had to work with was not enough, and asked to be taken off the project, but due to time constraints there was no choice for him other than to stay.

'I said, '"Look, let's go for it and do something that's completely weird ... Let's do something that nobody's ever tried before, and really surprise the audience," and in a way, what Bob came up with, when you think about the Doctor being plugged into the computer, was actually a sort of precursor to virtual reality.' **Hinchcliffe**

This pressure led to him leaving the BBC after the first recording block had been staged, from August 15th to 17th in TC3, and Joan Ellacott was assigned to the serial to take over for the last few days of production, working with Maloney to keep everything on line.

THE DEADLY ASSASSIN:
George Pravda as Castellan
Spandrell and Bernard
Horsfall as Chancellor
Goth, discussing the fate
of the Doctor

Hinchcliffe was pleased with the director's work. 'If you look at any of David's shows, even the studio-bound ones like "Planet of Evil", you can see that he keeps the camera moving all the time, and he edits the material quite vigorously. He always manages to keep a sense of movement and energy throughout his stories.'

Music was a key element, according to Hinchcliffe. 'The Time Lords were difficult to portray because you couldn't make them completely hi-tech, and it would have been wrong to go for a mysterious and mystical approach, but as a whole the overall design and mix of background music made something that was quite successful.

'Dudley Simpson always responded to the central thrust and concept of a programme. I would give him a full and very comprehensive briefing, not only about what we'd accomplished in the finished programme but also about what the original intentions of the story were, so that he had the core inspiration in his mind. I spoke to him as I did to the designers; I had a very close working relationship with him.

'Any. story's dub session was important because it was your last chance to try and remedy anything that hadn't worked out in the studio. Dudley could always come up with something to boost a story when it was flagging, and manage to knit all the studio material together with his linking themes.'

'The Deadly Assassin' came to an end with

'I remember David Maloney saying that he had this idea that the Time Lords would parade around in their ceremonies with a very decorative style of robing, with a fanned out collar behind their heads like a peacock displaying its plumage. I don't know whether the costume designer actually took the motif from David, but once he told me I couldn't really look at them without chuckling to myself at the idea he'd put in my head.' **Holmes**

THE DEADLY ASSASSIN:
Baker during rehearsals on
the prison cell set, being
tortured by Derek Seaton
as Commander Hildred

a final two-day studio block in TC8, working across September 1st and 2nd. Maloney was asked at this point whether he'd be willing to return for the season's finale and handle the proposed six-part story that would bring the year's run of productions to a close. He agreed, and came back to rejoin the production team in mid-October, when pre-production was due to begin.

The story in question had been commissioned by Holmes in January from Robert Banks Stewart, who was developing the project under the working title of 'The Foe from the Future'. The only other writers under consideration for Season Fourteen were Basil Dawson, whose Victorian-based 'The Gaslight Murders' was due to be made after 'The Deadly Assassin' until it fell through at scripting stage, bringing a new writer to the series by the name of Chris Boucher.

Boucher had been submitting ideas to the programme for the past couple of years, and Holmes had really worked on nurturing them to see if anything could reach the standards required to make it as far as production. Hinchcliffe also fed the process:

'A notion I'd come up with for a story was given to Chris by Bob. He was really Bob's discovery, and became the closest one of our writers to be able to approximate the style that Bob had developed for writing *Doctor Who*.

THE FACE OF EVIL: Baker on the set of the Savateem's main council hut

THE FACE OF EVIL: Leon Eagles as Jabel, with Baker and Peter Baldock as an Acolyte

'I wanted to do a story where the Doctor, at some point in the past, has visited a planet and unwittingly had a devastating effect on its society, which he has to set right on a return journey. The idea of how quickly man can degenerate from his previous set of beliefs to a new, more primitive set of values, which are slightly askew, was one that fascinated me.

'Chris wanted to do an idea where a god or a computer runs amok, so Bob instigated the notion of merging the two together. You always needed a really powerful hook with a story concept, which would pull your audience through until at least episode three. There had to be an overridingly powerful mystery at the heart of each adventure which gave it momentum and energy, and it had to have a very clear logic all the way through. That was one of our strengths, and it really showed through in "The Face of Evil" …'

Boucher's original idea had already been through two attempts at getting it right, as 'The Mentor Conspiracy' and 'The Dreamers of Phados', and when he began work on the new augmented version he came up with the potentially inflammatory working title of 'The Day God Went Mad'. But Holmes had faith in him.

'Chris Boucher was a great find as far as the programme was concerned. He was brimming with energy, full of enthusiasm and had an imagination that operated on the same level as mine … and, apart from anything else, he was working for Calor Gas at the time, so that sold him to me in an instant.'

'The Face of Evil' took over the production slot left by 'The Gaslight Murders', which had been dropped quite early on, so Hinchcliffe knew there was a gap that had to be filled. Holmes did not have time to write another script himself as he was already committed to writing a new finale for the season from scratch. Banks Stewart had to abandon his story while he was still developing the plot, and using one or two of his basic ideas Holmes was at work on 'The Talons of Weng-Chiang', with David Maloney helping to structure it as work progressed. As it turned out, Boucher would be called to step into the breach.

There were other holes to be filled, notably the absence of a companion for the Doctor. But, as Hinchcliffe relates, 'We were beginning to attract some of the top talent within the BBC to the show: Austin Ruddy was an inspired designer and John Bloomfield was a great costume designer … New blood was coming in. I was looking around for other directors because I couldn't rely on the "old reliables" all of the time, and it was really Pennant Roberts, who came on board to direct "The Face of Evil", who pushed for Louise Jameson to get the role of Leela, as she had all of the attributes we were looking for.'

At the beginning of the season, Hinchcliffe and Holmes had begun to formulate specific ideas over the character they wanted as the new companion. Hinchcliffe sets out their ideas:

'We came up with this notion of using a sort of Eliza Doolittle character: an uncouth cockney girl, who the Doctor would meet in the Victorian story and take on board the TARDIS. She was going to

THE FACE OF EVIL: Baker, with Brendan Price as Tomas, with Louise Jameson as Leela and Leslie Schofield as Calib on the ground before them

THE FACE OF EVIL: Baker forces Price and Schofield to lift Jameson onto a couch, as the Doctor races to save Leela from the poison of a janus thorn

THE FACE OF EVIL: Leela and Tomas are flanked by two Savateem Guards as they are held captive

THE FACE OF EVIL: Tom Baker on set, opposite left, during the staging of the film sequences for the story, which were carried out at Ealing Film Studios

Jameson pictured during a press call for Season Fifteen, opposite right, after the decision had been made to keep her character on long-term

'My idea was to have a sharper relationship between Leela and the Doctor than occurred in her first two stories, and that only began to appear when Bob wrote for her in the final story of that season. She was meant to be always catching the Doctor off guard. She killed people with her dagger and the poisonous thorns, which really infuriated him.' **Hinchcliffe**

be a bright, cheeky personality, who gave the Doctor a lot of lip. So there would be a Professor Higgins/Eliza relationship between them, which would give conflict and an edge to all their scenes together.'

Holmes was keen to do a Victorian story which was a pastiche of all the old Fu Manchu films, but with the commitments he had to 'The Deadly Assassin' he was unable to, and Dawson's script attempted to address this idea. But, when that fell through, the companion introduction had to be worked into Boucher's script.

Holmes: 'We told Chris that we had to work the new girl into his story, and suddenly realised that the basic concept of the relationship we had in mind would work even better between the Doctor and a primitive warrior.'

Filming began at Ealing for 'The Face of Evil' on September 20th and lasted for seven days. During early drafting stages on the script, Boucher had written two endings, Leela either leaving with the Doctor or remaining on her home planet. Just prior to the start of shooting, he was told that the character would appear in at least one more story, which he was also asked to write.

The contingency plan Hinchcliffe had was to see if Leela worked out over the course of eight episodes, and if not leave her out of the series at the end of Boucher's second script, and then bring in the cockney character in Holmes's Fu Manchu epic that he was working on.

Some of the actresses who auditioned for the part of Leela included Emily Richards, Carol Drinkwater, Colette Gleeson, Carol Leader, Belinda Law, Sally Geeson, Susan Wooldridge and Pamela Salem, who went on to win a part in 'The Robots of Death', which Boucher started work on under the title of 'The Storm Mine Murders' with little under four weeks to complete the story before it was due to go into pre-production.

Studio recording started on October 11th, and ran until October 12th in TC3; the story was completed in the same venue on October 25th and the 26th.

Transmission deadlines were by now beginning to catch up with the production team, and Hinchcliffe managed to gain a brief period of respite for the recording schedules when it was agreed that there would be a gap of six weeks between 'The Deadly Assassin' and 'The Face of Evil', so instead of starting on November 27th, Leela's debut on screen was postponed until New Year's Day 1977.

On November 2nd Michael E. Briant started to direct some of the film sequences at the Ealing studios for 'The Robots of Death', with four days of shooting lasting until November 5th. There had not actually been many robot -orientated stories in the history of the programme, and it was a balance that the producer was keen to redress.

'I told Bob Holmes that I wanted to do a very sophisticated robot story, and he said that it would have to be set in a self-contained environment. I didn't want it to be yet another space station, so I suggested a mineral digger. I went to see Richard Conway, who'd achieved such good model filming results on "The Seeds of Doom", and asked if he could make something that would convey a sense of scale without looking like a piece of cardboard that was wobbling around.'

Holmes comments, 'Philip had absorbed a huge amount of pulp science fiction, and you could see that Asimov's robot stories had stuck in his mind, as had the more bizarre Philip K. Dick novels, and "The Robots of Death" certainly had more than a hint of Frank Herbert [author of *Dune*] about it.'

Hinchcliffe explains that his 'notion' was 'to have something go wrong with the robots on board this immense vessel, and it was Chris Boucher and Bob who dreamed up the far more disciplined idea of doing it as an Agatha Christie story, with people mysteriously being bumped off, one after the other ...

'I think I had a bit of a preoccupation with having a companion that was like Raquel Welch in One Million Years BC, *complete with fur-lined bikini. We really wanted to aggravate the Doctor's morals by having him approach an apparent threat with peaceful intentions and a willingness to talk the situation through, only to find that Leela throws a spear through it before he has a chance to say anything ... John Bloomfield's costume for her wasn't quite the fur-lined apparition I had in mind, but it certainly gave rise to a few wolf whistles when Louise first walked into the studio, and you can be sure of one thing: she really told the guilty technicians what she thought of them, and they didn't make another sound. It might have been something to do with her dagger!'*
Holmes

THE ROBOTS OF DEATH:
David Collings as Poul,
Pamela Salem as Toos and
Brian Croucher as Borg
during a break in
rehearsals, with two of the
extras playing Robots
taking a break from
wearing their masks in the
background

THE ROBOTS OF DEATH:
the main cast, bar Baker
and Jameson, on the
recreation chamber set

'I'd originally envisaged the robots as being something completely different to the Cybermen, for example. They had to be gleaming, glistening and hi-tech. Michael and his design team hit on the idea that the crew of this ship, with all the time they had to kill until they found an ore stream, would be rather effete, with a luxurious environment around themselves.

'This spilt over into the way the robots might be built. Why have ones that were so obviously mechanical when they could be aesthetically pleasing instead? I was actually against the art deco look at first, but I was eventually won over and just accepted that this was going to be something radically different.'

Remembering his first sight of the robot costumes, Holmes says that 'the immediate concern was over whether these things would actually have any "scare quality" to them. Michael came up with this elaborate form of choreographed movement for them which, when you mixed them with these calm and collected voices, created quite a sinister effect. That wouldn't have worked at all if Michael had gone with a typical, clichéd robot look.'

Briant took the unusual step of using the first day of both the recording blocks he was allocated on this story

THE ROBOTS OF DEATH: Richard Seager in full costume as V3

THE ROBOTS OF DEATH: David Collings as Poul, alongside the deceased Cass, Tariq Yunus, on one of the crew's bedroom sets

THE ROBOTS OF DEATH:
The elaborate set for the
Conning Tower's main
Control Room on board
the Sandminer

to do camera rehearsals. As a consequence, the following day had a very tense schedule to complete. The first block was staged in TC3 on November 22nd and 23rd.

Hinchcliffe reports that 'Michael was extremely inventive in terms of using CSO [Colour Separation Overlay] in the studio, such as the sequence where you close in towards the model of the sand-miner, and can actually see the conning tower control room with people moving about inside. That was about the height of the tricks we could achieve on the budgets that we had. He shot all that stuff extremely well.

'"The Robots of Death" managed to fulfil all of its story intentions; it doesn't attempt to do anything that it can't accomplish, and you can actually say that about very few *Doctor Who* serials. This had to be one of the best stories of my three seasons, and it was almost an unqualified success.'

Holmes adds that 'Michael and Philip had not seen eye to eye over the last story he'd done, and the general view was that "Revenge of the Cybermen" had missed the mark entirely. This was not a reflection on Michael, because he was full of enthusiasm and inventive ideas, but you'd hardly think that "The Robots of Death" had been directed by the same man. That's the nature of *Doctor Who*, even for the writers: sometimes you have hits, sometimes you have misses.'

THE ROBOTS OF DEATH:
Eight Robot costumes were
built in all, with the illusion
of a far greater number
being achieved by
swapping number plates
around on each actor, so
they each played between
one to four Robots

THE ROBOTS OF DEATH:
Louise Jameson and
Pamela Salem surrounded
by Robots, during a break
in rehearsals

The second studio session ran for three days, with the crew remaining in TC3 from December 5th, which was the camera rehearsal day, to December 7th, when 'The Robots of Death' wrapped. With rehearsals now due to begin on 'The Talons of Weng-Chiang', Holmes had only managed to complete final drafts of the first four episodes by that point. Hinchcliffe stepped in.

'For a time there was a risk that Bob wasn't going to do the story, mainly because he had so much on and he was also basically worn out. I went to David Maloney and asked him whether we'd be able to get pre-production underway by knowing just the basics of what we'd need from the storyline, in the absence of completed scripts, and he said that it was possible. So I was able to extend the deadline for completing it, which helped me to persuade Bob to do it.'

With Holmes planning the concluding two episodes to be entirely studio bound, Maloney was able to get the location material needed for the first four parts underway. There was a longer period available for this, compared to normal six-parters, because Hinchcliffe had done a trade-off and swapped one of the three studio recording blocks allocated to the story for more location time.

Eight days of filming were staged around various sites in London from December 13th to the 20th, starting with night shooting around the old dock areas and wharfs in Wapping, before moving to Twickenham, where a suitably preserved Victorian street in Cambridge Park was used.

But there were problems with the script, as Hinchcliffe explains. 'There wasn't a sense early enough of exactly who the main protagonist was. There's something wrong in the storytelling, because we just don't realise exactly how powerful this man is, or what he's going to do. Some of that is my fault …

THE ROBOTS OF DEATH: A
special effects sequence
underway, as one of the
Robots explodes in Taren
Capel's laboratory

THE TALONS OF WENG-CHIANG: Trevor Baxter, seated, as Professor Litefoot with Baker standing alongside him, on the set of Litefoot's dining room

THE TALONS OF WENG-CHIANG: In keeping with the spirit of Robert Holmes's script being an affectionate tribute to the Boy's Own spirit of storytelling, Baker was given a suitably Holmesian (as in Sherlock) costume for the story

'In early drafts of the story Bob wanted the character to be the Master, and I objected to that strongly because I felt it was an abrogation of originality. I didn't want to go down the route of having the Master turning out to be the villain again. Even so, in the finished story all the clues are there which quite clearly point to the fact that it should have been him.'

This revelation would have come with the cliffhanger of part five where Leela tears Greel's mask away, and the audience would have seen the decaying features that were so familiar from 'The Deadly Assassin'. The time cabinet, distilling the life essence of people to be able to survive, etcetera – it all clearly points towards the Master. Holmes details the cause of the scripts' shortcomings.

'The reason that the scripts for 'Weng-Chiang' had to be written so quickly was simply that I'd been on holiday abroad, and my wife was taken ill and had to spend quite a while in hospital. I didn't get back to the office until about three weeks later than planned, and that was the first time I found out about Robert Banks Stewart having to back out of the final story. I was very tired and wasn't that keen on doing a whole new batch of scripts from scratch, but Philip is a master of persuasion so I got to do a take on Fu Manchu after all.'

A further eight days of location work began shortly after the new year, with the cast and crew travelling up to

Northampton, where the Repertory Theatre there was used to double for the Palace Theatre in the story. Maloney was now using outside broadcast cameras in favour of film, and sequences were staged in an abandoned rates office, which doubled as the interior of the police headquarters, and also St Crispin's Hospital in Dunston, where scenes involving Chang's dressing room and Litefoot's mortuary were realised.

For the variety act sequences, which involved a dozen or so extras to fill the front row of the stalls in the theatre, a cameo appearance was made by Dudley Simpson, complete with tail-suit, as the conductor in the orchestra pit.

Hinchcliffe, however, noticed that something was changing. 'Somehow, the edges of Leela's character were becoming softened, and although it probably made her more sympathetic and attractive to the

audience, it actually weakened the initial concept. We really wanted her to be this total barbarian, who was quite shocking. Maybe 50 to 60 per cent of the role as we envisaged it came across, and then Louise brought something else of her own personality to the part we couldn't have foreseen. Without wishing to criticise her in any way, there was a difference between how we'd planned out Leela and how Louise eventually emerged.'

THE TALONS OF WENG-CHIANG: Michael Spice as Magnus Greel, alias Weng-Chiang, minus his leather mask, during rehearsals in the Dragon Room set, in the latter stages of studio recording for Episode Five and Six of the story

THE TALONS OF WENG-CHIANG: Louise Jameson and Tom Baker in the sewer set, which was built within the confines of the studio rather than film the sequences in an authentic drainage system

THE TALONS OF WENG-CHIANG: Louise Jameson as Leela, drying out in Litefoot's dining room, after facing a giant rat...

'I don't know how influential Tom was in this, because by this time I began to sense that there was a bit of aggravation between the two of them. I wasn't aware of any deep-rooted animosity, but things certainly began to break out while we were in Northampton. I was told that Tom was being extremely difficult with her, and that she'd got terribly upset, but it never came to a confrontation between myself and Tom, although I did look into the matter to see what I could do. David was such an experienced director that he was able to defuse the situation and get them to get on with the job at hand. Maybe the real give and take that you expect to exist between an actor and actress, which helps make a scene work, just wasn't quite happening between them.'

After recording from January 7th to 14th, everyone returned to London and rehearsals began for the first studio session, which ran from January 24th to 25th 1977. The sewer sets were erected in TC8, and as Hinchcliffe recalls, 'We had problems with the water which was leaking, and in the lunch hour we were told that we were causing havoc with the phone lines. Because Bob had written these giant rats into the story, there was talk in the early planning stages about using trained rats against a CSO background, but we decided they were not reliable enough to do what the story demanded on cue. So the decision was made to make a life size "giant" costume, to be worn and operated by Stuart Fell. In theory this was fine, but something was slightly wrong – the fur was too clean, the teeth seemed wrong and, after realising this, in the early stages of recording David used close-ups on the rat's eyes instead.'

During rehearsals for the second recording block, a camera crew from The Lively Arts, who were making a documentary called 'Who's Doctor Who...', trailed the production team in the run up to the next three days in studio, which ran from February 8th to the 10th. As recording began to draw to a close on the last day, things started to go wrong, as Hinchcliffe relates:

'We were supposed to finish at ten o'clock, as per normal, and the special effects designer, Michaeljohn Harris, had rigged up all the furniture in the Dragon Hall to explode on cue, as the laser bolts from the Dragon prop's eyes hit them, but when we got to that sequence none of the explosive charges went off. None of them functioned at all, so David Maloney took charge of the whole thing and jumped ahead of schedule to do what he could while they were rigged up again.

'It was a special effects man's nightmare, when everything goes wrong like that. There was no way we could get everything done in time, so I had to go down to the studio floor and negotiate with each member of the crew individually, to see if they were willing to go into overtime. By the time we got to half past ten some of them started to walk out, and we were left operating with a reduced crew. Eventually, we finished at twenty to eleven, and that was my last ever recording day as the producer of *Doctor Who*.'

The news of Hinchcliffe's departure from the programme was a surprise to everybody ... even to Hinchcliffe himself ...

THE TALONS OF WENG-CHIANG: The Doctor searches through the sewers, armed with Professor Litefoot's elephant gun. The story not only marked the end of Series Fourteen, but also the end of the Hincclffe era as a whole...

Chapter Six

Lost Horizons

'There were ideas and themes that we
never got a chance to explore …
everything was cut short when they
moved Philip on to pastures new …'
Robert Holmes   Interviewed March 1985

THERE WAS NEVER a meeting giving him the opportunity to say what his thoughts on the matter were. There was no prior warning. There was no choice. The first thing that Hinchcliffe knew about the fact that he was being moved on to another series was when his successor walked into the *Doctor Who* production office, sat down and told him that he was taking over his job.

'Graham Williams literally breezed in and told me that he was taking over. This was a hell of a shock because I had no idea whatsoever that this was going to happen. Of course, I was angry that none of the heads of the Drama Department had bothered to tell me, but I kept calm and told Graham that he'd better start trailing me.

'There were still a couple of stories to go in Season Fourteen, and I explained that heading the programme could be a difficult job, and that I'd trailed Barry Letts for quite some time before I got the hang of it. I mean, if I had been in Graham's situation I would have been following me like a hawk . . . but that was the last I saw of him.

Holmes explains. 'When you were a staff member at the BBC you could be moved from programme to programme at a moment's notice. Philip suddenly found out what it was like to be a pawn in a chess game. It was a bit of a bombshell to drop on him, and there was no apparent rationale behind it.

'Philip eventually resigned himself to the fact that it was better to go out on top. The ratings were high, and thanks to *Doctor Who* he had a hell of a reputation within the BBC … although, I think the slightly underhand way he was treated did leave a bit of a sour aftertaste in his mouth.'

Holmes decided to leave at the same point as Hinchcliffe, but eventually agreed to stay on for a further four months when Williams arrived, just to get the first few scripts of the year in order.

Therefore, 'The Talons of Weng-Chiang' marked the end of an era, and in an ironic twist, Hinchcliffe moved on to produce *Target*, a hard-edged crime thriller series that Williams had actually devised.

For a brief time it actually seemed as though Hinchcliffe and Holmes would be staying on for a fourth year. Shortly after the producer was told he was leaving, the decision was reversed for about a week, and ideas began to start forming between the two of them over what they wanted to do with stories for Season Fifteen but, of course, this never happened.

'I seem to recall sitting down and chatting over a few thoughts and notions,' says Holmes, 'but nothing was ever put down on paper, although the ideas were certainly beginning to brew.'

Rather than live in the past shadows of such regular foes as the Daleks and Cybermen, Hinchcliffe was prepared to commit some time to developing a new race of creatures for the unfilmed season, as he explains:

'I had a hankering to come up with something just as memorable as the Daleks, and I kept badgering Bob about this idea, and spoke to designers about it, like Roger Murray-Leach. The idea had come from the image of the Ku-Klux-Klan with their cone-like hoods, but this was a creature that was the colour of ebony, and not their pristine white.

'Overall, it was like a smooth, black chess-piece, which would have a wider base and a slightly bowed body, which would come up to this high-pointed head.

'The whole thing would have an obelisk-like quality, with no human features at all, but just smooth indentations to suggest some sort of shape. It was a silicon-based life-form which would silently glide around using the 'Davros' principle. I guess they would have had some kind of voice, but I hadn't got as far as figuring out how they could communicate.

'Anyway, I drew these things, and kept showing them to Bob and saying, "Can't we get anyone to write a story using something like this?" but nobody ever seemed to get the point. These things weren't going to trundle round like Daleks, they'd do something far more eerie. I wanted these creatures to have a high scare factor in the way they were realised.'

With 'The Masque of Mandragora' and 'The Talons of Weng-Chiang', a format had successfully been established for using historical earth settings and imposing an alien threat on them which the Doctor then had to defeat. It was a style of serial that both Hinchcliffe and Holmes were keen to pursue.

Hinchcliffe was enthusiastic. 'We were beginning to generate a rather John Buchanesque, almost colonial feel to the stories. Tom was becoming a man of action, his was a very physical Doctor, compared to the ones before. There were ideas like taking him to the Boer War or into the depths of the rain forests in Brazil.

'I called it the Kennedy Theory, which simply involved getting writers thinking along the lines of twisting history by saying, "What if it was a Dalek on the grassy knoll?"' **Holmes**

'Douglas Camfield kept telling me to read the Sword and Sorcery novels, saying, "Philip, you have to get into these. They're going to be big!" At first I didn't believe him, but I began to see what he was getting at. I had an instinct that the type of Boys' Own hero of old was going to become fashionable again, and *Raiders of the Lost Ark* proved how right I was.

Tom Baker during his time as the presenter of The Book Tower, *a series he recorded alongside* Doctor Who...

'The Indiana Jones territory was very much the kind of area we would have taken the series into. We'd have taken Tom into the *King Solomon's Mines*/H. Rider Haggard area. Bob wanted to do something like Joseph Conrad's *Heart of Darkness*, but give it a *Doctor Who* slant.'

Holmes remembers another story.

'Philip and I did come up with this idea of having Tom land in the lost city of the Incas just as the first team of English explorers found it at the end of the 1800s, so they immediately became suspicious of him, and the Doctor discovers that this gold temple at the heart of the city is actually a vast type of transmat … Then something – I don't know what – was going to beam down and start killing these explorers off, one by one …'

Hinchcliffe continues:

'The historical stories would have been combined with a couple of high-concept sci-fi stories, but purely for logistical reasons there would have been some stories in a more up-to-date, contemporary setting as well. The challenge would have been to do these in an original way, so that they didn't end up as typical invasion of Earth stories.

'There were no particular plans to bring UNIT back, but there was certainly no hard rule to say that they would never be seen again. Basically, Bob and I had skipped over that kind of story because Barry Letts had done so many of them, but that doesn't mean that the Brigadier would never have been seen again. Nick Courtney was certainly keen to know whether there was a future for him with the programme.'

As far as the state of the travelling companions for the Doctor was concerned, Hinchcliffe had every intention of keeping Louise Jameson on for all of Season Fifteen, as he explains:

'The situation between her and the Doctor would have been brought to a head during the next season, with him saying, "Look, you can't go on behaving like a savage," and she would have then done something dramatic to save his life by doing exactly that. The whole question of her primitive sensibilities would have been in conflict with the Doctor's sense of morality.

'We would have introduced a young man in one story, who would have taken a – shall we say – interest in Leela, but in no way would it have been overstated. I think we would have explored the fact that she didn't realise that she could have that kind of effect on people.

'The story would have been one of the historical ones, with the man behaving according to the manners of the period, while she was behaving in a rather outré fashion. We would have introduced a great deal more conflict with the Doctor as the stories progressed, with his attitude becoming harsher and far ruder, a bit like Professor Higgins with Eliza Doolittle.

'In a way, the Doctor would have been becoming very fond of her, but just couldn't allow himself to admit that this was the case. There was no sexual connotation to this at all, she was just a loyal and faithful companion. He would have allowed her annoyance factor to anger him, and ignored the qualities she had of bravery and courage, so we would have engineered a scene where he had to come face to face with this fact.

'The ill-tempered, bombastic side of the Doctor's personality would have shown through, and there would have been a real problem for him to admit that he cared. The relationship would have gone on to a deeper level, and he would have realised that she was someone that he should value more highly. Despite all the shouting about taking her back and dumping her on her home planet whenever she did anything wrong, it had to be quite clear that he would never actually bring himself to do that, and in a way Leela would have realised this as well.'

'It would have been interesting to have Tom wander down the TARDIS corridor looking for her,' adds Holmes, 'and find her in a quiet corner doing something like trying to teach herself to read, or trying to do a simple drawing with a pencil. The Doctor would never have taken it off her and shown her how to do it. I think we'd have had Tom look slightly surprised,

Baker during a press call for Season Fifteen, which marked the beginning of Graham Williams' tenure as Producer of Doctor Who

Hinchcliffe's plans for Season Fifteen would have entailed increasing the heroic nuances of the Doctor's character

pleased for her, and then just have him creep away without saying a single word.'

Elaborate science fiction concepts were also being considered, with ideas running along a more plausible thread such as had been established with 'The Robots of Death'. There was a hard edge of what Holmes liked to call 'the impossibly probable' behind the central ideas. Hinchcliffe sketches some of the possibilities.

'One idea was to have a gigantic spaceship, which contained its own environment, with gardens and cities, and it was on an epic journey so that generations of the crew had come and gone. The Doctor would find that the crew are now the great-great-grandchildren of the original team, and that some breakdown in their society had taken place …

'Another notion – for one of the modern day Earth stories – would be to have had the TARDIS land in London, or some major city, and have the Doctor find that the sky is practically blotted out by an enormous spaceship like in 'Childhood's End'. Normal life was continuing, but with an awful sort of alien enslavement that humans could do nothing about.'

It's all a case of what might have been, but these ideas illustrate the kind of route that Hinchcliffe and Holmes would have headed along. One thing is certain, and that's that both men agreed they could not have asked for a more enthusiastic actor as their Doctor.

Hinchcliffe: 'I was certainly very satisfied with Tom's performance all the way through. He grasped the fact that the role made him a kind of folk hero, and he went to great lengths to preserve the image of the Doctor in his private life. He was all too aware of the problems his name splattered across the headlines would have caused for the series' reputation.'

Holmes: 'Tom wasn't just reading the lines on cue. This was an actor who wanted to become the character and absorb every aspect of his being. That may sound a bit extreme, but all you have to do is look at the stories we made to see what kind of results that can achieve.'

The end of Season Fourteen did not mark the end of the working relationship between Hinchcliffe and Holmes, because they were soon developing another science fiction project together, intent on teaming up as a producer/writer partnership once again as Hinchcliffe relates.

'We always thought that it would be good if we could come up with another sort of *Quatermass*-type series, and we concocted this idea between us called *Lituvin 40*. Graeme McDonald had by then taken over as the BBC's Head of Drama Series and Serials and he was very keen on the idea, and Bob was very close to getting commissioned, but it all fell through.

'I think it would have been a very good, contemporary science fiction story. There was

Hinchcliffe wanted the Doctor to become a figure that was akin to the heros of the novels of H.G. Wells and Jules Verne, so the Time Lord would become more and more like a Victorian adventurer...

Although UNIT had been phased out during his time, Hinchcliffe did not rule out the possibility of their return in Season Fifteen, or another appearance by the Brigadier, opposite bottom

also talk of spinning off the Jago and Litefoot characters from 'The Talons of Weng-Chiang' so that they got their own series. It would have been sort of *X-Files* in the 1890s, and although Bob wrote a draft script it didn't come to anything.'

Hinchcliffe was left feeling that they had been involved in something significant.

'With hindsight, I do feel we were part of the movement that was starting to bring science fiction back with a bang at that time. It was only a couple of years or so before *Star Wars* appeared. I watched with fascination when all these movies like *Alien*, *Blade Runner*, *The Empire Strikes Back* and *The Terminator* started to appear.

'These were certainly the areas where I was beginning to think in. Perhaps, without realising it at the time, Bob and I were sensitive to what audiences would go for, and what was unfurling in terms of story areas and effects in the future.

'I think we were part of a larger movement which quickly accelerated towards the end of the 1970s and ran throughout the course of the 1980s. Science fiction became huge again, and it was no longer B-movie material, they were trying to tell the same kind of stories as we were.

'Perhaps Bob and I should have gone to Hollywood ...'

Cast & Crew Listings

Notes: *All stories are listed in broadcast order, and not in order of production. The story codes allocated to each production have been noted in brackets alongside the story titles.*
'Robot', Tom Baker's debut story, although a part of Season 12, has been excluded from the listing, as the producer was Barry Letts and not Philip Hinchcliffe.

Season Twelve

Regular Cast

Doctor Who ....Tom Baker
Sarah Jane Smith...Elisabeth Sladen
Harry Sullivan...Ian Marter

Regular Production Team

Producer ....Philip Hinchcliffe
Script Editor ....Robert Holmes
Production Unit Manager ....George Gallaccio
Special Sound..Dick Mills
Title Sequence ....Bernard Lodge

Title Music by Ron Grainer and the BBC Radiophonic Workshop

The Ark in Space
(Story 4C)
(4 Episodes)

Written by Robert Holmes

Vira...Wendy Williams
Noah..Kenton Moore
Libri...Christopher Masters
Lycett...John Gregg
Rogin ....Richardson Morgan
High Minister's Voice ....Gladys Spencer
Voices..Peter Tuddenham
Wirrn Operators ....Stuart Fell, Nick Hobbs
Wirrn Grub Operator ....Stuart Fell
Dune ....Brian Jacobs
Bodies In Pallets............................Jan Goram,
Barry Summerford, Rick Carroll,
Roy Brent, Richard Archer, Sean
Cooner, Peter Duke, Geoffrey Brighty,
Lyn Summer, Tina Roach

Production Credits

Production Assistant....................Marion McDougall
Assistant Floor Manager ....Russ Karel
Studio Lighting....................................Nigel Wright
Studio Sound ....John Lloyd
Senior Studio Cameraman..................Peter Granger
Costume Design ....Barbara Kidd
Make-Up Design ....Sylvia James
Visual Effects...........John Friedlander & Tony Oxley
Designer ....Roger Murray-Leach
Incidental Music ....Dudley Simpson
Director ....Rodney Bennett

The Sontaran Experiment
(Story 4B)
(2 Episodes)

Written by Bob Baker & Dave Martin

Erak ....Peter Walshe
Krans ....Glyn Jones
Vural ....Donald Douglas
Roth ....Peter Rutherford
Zake......................................Terry Walsh
Field-Major Styre.........................Kevin Lindsay
Prisoner..................................Brian Ellis
The Marshal ....Kevin Lindsay
Stunt Double for Doctor Who
& Harry Sullivan ....Terry Walsh
Stunt Double for Field-Major Styre............Stuart Fell

Production Credits

Production Assistant.....................Marion McDougall
Assistant Floor Manager ....Russ Karel
Outside Broadcast Unit Lighting.......Tommy Thomas
Outside Broadcast Unit Sound...............Vic Godrich
Costume Design.......................Barbara Kidd
Make-Up Design ....Sylvia James
Visual Effects............John Friedlander & Tony Oxley
Designer ....Roger Murray-Leach
Incidental Music ....Dudley Simpson
Director ....Rodney Bennett

Genesis of the Daleks
(Story 4E)
(6 Episodes)

Written by Terry Nation

Time Lord ....John Franklin-Robbins
Kaled Leader ....Richard Reeves
General Ravon ....Guy Siner
Security Commander Nyder ....Peter Miles
Gharman...........................Dennis Chinnery
Davros.......................................Michael Wisher
Sevrin ....Stephen Yardley
Ronson.................................James Garbutt
Tane.......................................Drew Wood
Gerril ....Jeremy Chandler
Thal Soldier ....Pat Gorman
Kavell.....................................Tom Georgeson
Mogren......................................Ivor Roberts
Thal Politician....................................Michael Lynch
Thal Soldier ....Hilary Minster
Bettan.......................................Harriet Philpin
Kaled Guard...Peter Mantle
Thal Soldier ....John Gleeson
Kaled Officer Kavos ....Andrew Johns
Kaled Boy...Paul Burton
Dalek Voices ....Roy Skelton with Michael Wisher
Daleks Operators ....John Scott Martin
                with Cy Town & Keith Ashley
Kaleds.......................................Tony O'Reefe,
        Steve Butler & Michael Brinker
Kaled Soldiers..................Peter Kodak, Giles Melville
Kaled Councillors....Anthony Lang, Ronald Nunnery,
                George Romanoff
Kaled Scientists..................Richard Orme, Pat Travis,
    Harry van Engel, William Ashley, Charles Erskine,
    John Timberlake, Charles Rayford, Alan Charles
    Thomas, Paddy Ryan, Terry Walsh, Mike Reynell,
                Tony Hayes
Kaled Guards.....................Alan Chuntz, Jim Dowdell
Kaled Prisoner..Ken Tracey
Kaled Soldier Stunt Double....................Alan Chuntz
Kaled Elite Guards ....Bob Watson, Giles Melville,
        Peter Kodak, Barry Summerford, Roy Caesar

Thals ....Dougal Rossiter, Kirk Klugston, Julian Peters
Thal Guards.................Terry Walsh, Patrick Scoular,
    Les Conrad, Philip Mather, Dinny Powell, Jim
  Dowdall, David Cleeve, David Billa, Tim Blackstone
Thal Officers..............David Roy Paul, Keith Norrish
Thal Politician..................................Peter Whittaker
Thal Generals ....Eric Rayner
                John Beardmore
Thal Soldiers..................Philip Mather, Rick Carroll,
    Patrick Scoular, Ryan Craven, Julian Hudson,
                David Cleeve
Thal Soldier Stunt Double.......................Terry Walsh
Mutos ....James Muir, Terry Walsh, Roger Salter
                John Delieu, Stephen Calcutt
Thing ....Dod Watson
Driver Guard ....John Dunn
Guards......................Barry Summerford, Roy Caesar
Walk-Ons ....Michael Crane, David Cleeve,
    Peter Duke, David Billa, Christopher Holmes,
    Reg Turner, Tim Blackstone, Julian Hudson,
                John Sowerbutt

Production Credits

Production Assistant.....................Rosemary Crowson
Assistant Floor Manager......................Karilyn Collier
Studio Lighting ....Duncan Brown
Studio Sound...................................Tony Millier
Senior Studio Cameraman....................Peter Granger
Location Sound ....Bill Meekums
Location Film Cameraman ....Elmer Cossey
Costume Design.......................Barbara Kidd
Make-Up Design ....Sylvia James
Visual Effects ....Peter Day
Davros Mask Design ....John Friedlander
Designer ....David Spode
Incidental Music ....Dudley Simpson
Director ....David Maloney

Revenge of the Cybermen
(Story 4D)
(4 Episodes)

Written by Gerry Davis

Lester	William Marlowe
Commander Stevenson	Ronald Leigh-Hunt
Kellman	Jeremy Wilkin
Vorus	David Collings
Magrik	Michael Wisher
Tyrum	Kevin Stoney
Sheprah	Brian Grellis
Cyberleader	Christopher Robbie
First Cyberman	Melville Jones
Cybermen	Pat Gorman, Tony Lord
Colville's Voice & Monitor's Voice	Michael Wisher
Monitor Voice	Michael E. Briant
Vogans	Barry Summerford, Cy Town, Roy Caesar, Harry Fielder, David Billa, Leslie Weekes
Walk-On	David Sulkin
Stuntmen	Terry Walsh & Alan Chuntz

Production Credits

Production Assistant	John Bradburn
Assistant Floor Manager	Russ Karel
Studio Lighting	Derek Slee
Studio Sound	Norman Bennett
Senior Studio Cameraman	Peter Granger
Location Sound	John Gatland
Location Film Cameraman	Elmer Cossey
Costume Design	Prue Handley
Make-Up Design	Cecile Hay-Arthur
Visual Effects	James Ward
Cybermen Costumes	The Alistair Bowtell Effects Company
Designer	Roger Murray-Leach
Incidental Music	Carey Blyton
Director	Michael E. Briant

Season Thirteen
Regular Cast

Doctor Who	Tom Baker
Sarah Jane Smith	Elisabeth Sladen
Harry Sullivan (4F & 4J only)	Ian Marter

Regular Production Team

Producer	Philip Hinchcliffe
Script Editor	Robert Holmes
Production Unit Managers	George Gallacio
	(4F & 4L, 4G with Janet Radenkovic)
	Janet Radenkovic
	(4H-4K, 4G with George Gallacio)
Special Sound	Dick Mills
Title Sequence	Bernard Lodge

Title Music by Ron Grainer and the BBC Radiophonic Workshop

Terror of the Zygons
(Story 4F)
(4 Episodes)

Written by Robert Banks Stewart

Brigadier Lethbridge-Stewart ....Nicholas Courtney
RSM Benton ....John Levene
Duke of Forgill & Broton.................John Woodnutt
Munro ....Hugh Martin
Huckle ....Tony Sibbald
Angus...Angus Lennie
The Caber ....Robert Russell
Sister Lamont ....Lillias Walker
Radio Operator............................Bruce Wightman
Corporal ....Bernard G. High
Zygons.......Keith Ashley, David Selby, Ronald Gough
Soldier..Peter Symonds
Private Jackson ....James Muir
UNIT Corporal ....Rowland Geall
UNIT Soldiers ....Barry Summerford, Patrick Ginter
UNIT Soldiers at Conference ....Barry Summerford,
                                                    Alan Clements
Zygon Voices............Robert Russell, & Lillias Walker

Production Credits

Production Assistant ....Edwina Craze
Assistant Floor Manager ....Rosemary Webb
Studio Lighting..John Dixon
Studio Sound ....Michael McCarthy
Senior Studio Cameraman....................Peter Granger
Location Sound..John Tellick
Location Film Cameraman ....Peter Hall
Costume Design ....James Acheson
Make-Up Design ....Sylvia James
Visual Effects ....John Horton
Designer ....Nigel Curzon
Incidental Music ....Geoffrey Burgon
Director ....Douglas Camfield

Planet of Evil
(Story 4H)
(4 Episodes)

Written by Louis Marks

Sorenson ....Frederick Jaeger
Vishinsky.....................................Ewan Solon
Salamar ....Prentis Hancock
Braun ....Terence Brook
Baldwin.......................................Tony McEwan
Morelli ....Michael Wisher
De Haan ....Graham Weston
Ponti...Louis Mahoney
O'Hara...Haydn Wood
Reig ....Melvyn Bedford
Anti-Matter Monster Operator ....Mike Lee Lane
Voice Of Ranjit ....Michael Wisher
Morestrans ....Alfred Costa, David Rolfe,
          Julian Hudson, Richard Eden, Peter Dukes
Anti-Man Figures..............Ray Knight, Douglas Stark
Stunt Double for
Doctor Who & Sorenson ....Terry Walsh
Stunt Doubles for Morestrans ....Terry Walsh,
                                                    Max Faulkner

Production Credits

Production Assistant ....Malachy Shaw Jones
Assistant Floor Manager.....................Karilyn Collier
Studio Lighting ....Brian Clemmet
Studio Sound...Tony Millier
Sound (Elstree shooting) ....Colin March
Cameraman (Elstree shooting) ....Kenneth MacMillan
Senior Studio Cameraman....................Peter Granger
Costume Design ....Andrew Ross
Make-Up Design ....Jenny Shircore
Visual Effects.....................................Dave Harvard
Designer ....Roger Murray-Leach
Incidental Music ....Dudley Simpson
Director ....David Maloney

Pyramids of Mars
(Story 4G)
(4 Episodes)

Written by Stephen Harris

(Robert Holmes & Lewis Greifer)

Marcus Scarman ....Bernard Archard
Ibrahim Namin.................................Peter Mayock
Doctor Warlock ....Peter Copley
Laurence Scarman ....Michael Sheard
Collins ....Michael Bilton
Ernie Clements................................George Tovey
Ahmed ....Vic Tablian
Sutekh ....Gabriel Woolf
First Mummy....................................Nick Burnell
Second Mummy..............................Melvyn Bedford
Third Mummy ....Kevin Selway
Egyptian Labourers ....Oscar Charles, Tony Alless
Golden Mummies............Kevin Selway, Nick Burnell
Voice of Horus ....Gabriel Woolf

Production Credits

Production Assistant........................Peter Grimwade
Assistant Floor Manager ....Paul Braithwaite
Studio Lighting ....Ron Koplick
Studio Sound ....Brian Hiles
Location Sound................................Andrew Boulton
Location Film Cameraman................M. A. C. Adams
Costume Design..................................Barbara Kidd
Make-Up Design...................................Jean Steward
Visual Effects ....Ian Scoones, John Friedlander
Designer...Christine Ruscoe
Incidental Music ....Dudley Simpson
Director ....Paddy Russell

The Android Invasion
(Story 4J)
(4 Episodes)

Written by Terry Nation

Guy Crayford ....Milton Johns
Corporal Adams.................................Max Faulkner
Styggron ....Martin Friend
Chedaki ....Roy Skelton
RSM Benton ....John Levene
Morgan ....Peter Welch
Colonel Faraday.................................Patrick Newell
Grierson..Dave Carter
Tessa ....Heather Emmanuel
Matthews...Hugh Lund
Kraal..Stuart Fell
Farmer..Walter Goodman
Young Farmhand...............................Simon Christie
Barmaid...Margaret McKenchie
Country Doctor..................................Freddie White
Students...................Mark Holmes, Martine Holland
Defence Centre Receptionist ....Barbara Bermel
Scanner Room Technician ....Richard King
Man in Defence Centre ....Cy Town
Android Service Mechanics.....................Roy Pearce,
     Henry Lindsay, Alan Jennings, Derek Hunt
UNIT Soldiers ....Alf Custer, Alan Clements,
     Keith Ashley, Mark Allington, Christopher Woods,
Roy Pearce, Clinton Morris, Patrick Milner, Terry
     Sartain, Peter Brace, Derek Hunt
Villagers on Lorry .....Betsy White, George Ballantine,
     Ian Elliott, Lewis Alexander, Sue Manners
Villager in Space Shell............................Keith Ashley
Double for Doctor Who ....Terry Walsh
Double for Sarah Jane Smith ....Joan Woodgate
Double for Styggron ....Stuart Fell
Stuntman ....Peter Brace

Production Credits

Production Assistant....................Marion McDougall
Assistant Floor Manager ....Felicity Trew
Studio Lighting ....Duncan Brown
Studio Sound...Alan Machin
Location Sound.....................................Doug Mawson
Location Film Cameraman......................Ken Newson
Costume Design ....Barbara Lane
Make-Up Design.................................Sylvia Thornton
Visual Effects ....Len Hutton
Kraal Mask Design ....John Friedlander
Designer ....Philip Lindley
Incidental Music ....Dudley Simpson
Director ....Barry Letts

The Brain of Morbius
(Story 4K)
(4 Episodes)

Written by Robin Bland
(Terrance Dicks with Robert Holmes)

Solon ....Philip Madoc
Condo ....Colin Fay
Ohica..Gilly Brown
Maren ....Cynthia Grenville
Voice of Morbius.................................Michael Spice
First Sister ....Veronica Ridge
Second Sister...Janie Kells
Third Sister ....Sue Bishop
Fourth Sister ....Gabrielle Mowbray
Kriz...John Scott Martin
Morbius Monster ....Stuart Fell
Headless Morbius Monster.......................Alan Crisp
Sisters ....Martine Holland, Alison Daumler,
    Karen Burch, Mary Burleigh, Tobina Mahon-Brown
Stunt Double for Sarah Jane Smith........Jennie Le Fre

On-Screen Faces During Mind Battle ....Tom Baker,
    William Hartnell, Patrick Troughton, Jon
    Pertwee, Philip Hinchliffe, Robert Holmes,
    Douglas Camfield, Graeme Harper, Robert
    Banks Stewart, Christopher Baker, George
    Gallacio, Christopher Barry

Production Credits

Production Assistant ....Carol Wiseman
Assistant Floor Manager ....Felicity Trew
Studio Lighting.......................................Peter Catlett
Studio Sound...Tony Millier
Costume Design ....L. Rowland Warne
Make-Up Design ....Jean McMillan
Visual Effects ....John Horton
Designer...Barry Newbery
Incidental Music ....Dudley Simpson
Director ....Christopher Barry

The Seeds of Doom
(Story 4L)
(6 Episodes)

Written by Robert Banks Stewart

Charles Winlett.....................................John Gleeson
Derek Moberley ....Michael McStay
John Stevenson......................................Hubert Rees
Richard Dunbar ....Kenneth Gilbert
Hargreaves ....Seymour Green
Harrison Chase ....Tony Beckley
Scorby...John Challis
Sir Colin Thackeray ....Michael Barrington
Arnold Keeler...Mark Jones
Doctor Chester.....................................Ian Fairbairn
Amelia Ducat..................................Sylvia Coleridge
Major Beresford....................................John Acheson
Sergeant Henderson ....Ray Barron
Chauffeur ....Alan Chuntz
Guard Leader...................................David Materman
Guards...............................Harry Fielder, Ian Elliott,
                Pat Gorman, Bryan Nolan
Secretary ....Keith Ashley

Marines......................Ronald Gough, Patrick Milner
Krynoid........................Ronald Gough, Keith Ashley
Krynoid Voice ....Mark Jones
Stunt Double for Doctor Who................Terry Walsh

Production Credits

Production Assistant ....Graeme Harper
Assistant Floor Manager ....Sue Shearman
Studio Lighting.......................................John Dixon
Studio Sound ....John Holmes
Location Lighting ....Clive Potter
Location Sound...................................Vic Goodrich
Location Film Cameraman ....Keith Hopper
Costume Design ....Barbara Lane
Make-Up Design....................................Ann Briggs
Visual Effects ....Richard Conway
Designers ....Roger Murray-Leach & Jeremy Bear
Incidental Music ....Geoffrey Burgon
Director ....Douglas Camfield

Season Fourteen

Regular Cast

Doctor Who ....Tom Baker
Sarah Jane Smith (4M & 4N Only) ....Elisabeth Sladen
Leela (4Q onwards)..Louise Jameson

Regular Production Team

Producer ....Philip Hinchcliffe
Script Editor ....Robert Holmes
Production Unit Manager..Chris D'Oyly John
Special Sound..Dick Mills
Title Sequence ....Bernard Lodge
Title Music by Ron Grainer and the BBC Radiophonic Workshop

The Masque of Mandragora

(Story 4M)
(4 Episodes)

Written by Louis Marks

Count Frederico................................John Laurimore
Captain Rossini ....Anthony Carrick
Giuliano ....Gareth Armstrong
Marco...Tim Piggot-Smith
Hieronymous ....Norman Jones
High Priest ....Robert James
Brother ....Brian Ellis
Soldier ....Pat Gorman
Guards..........................John Clamp, James Appleby
Titan Voice ....Peter Tuddenham
Entertainer ....Stuart Fell
Pikemen ....Peter Walshe, Jay Neill, Cy Town,
                                             Leslie Weekes
Dancers..........................Kathy Wolff, Jack Edwards,
        Peggy Dixon, Alistair Fullarton, Michael Reid
Brethren........Walter Henry, Cy Town, Leslie Weekes,
       Roy Pearce, Keith Norrish, Clive Rogers, Pat
     Gorman, Dennis Plenty, Terry Sartain, James Muir,
                                             Keith Ashley
Extras.................Maurice Quick, Michael Mulcaster,
    Barbara Bernell, Jill Goldston, David Glynn Rogers,
    Colin Ianson, Lionel Taylor, Penny Lambirth, Kevin
    Moran, Mary Rennie, Martin Grant, Eddie Sommer,
      Martin Clarke, George Ballantine, Derek Chafer,
      Neville Ware, Jess Willard, Sheila Vivian, Jean
    Channon, Paul Barton, Christopher Holmes, Clinton
    Morris, David Wilde, David Rolfe, Lincoln Wright,
                                             Ken Tracey
Stuntmen ....Stuart Fell, Tex Fuller,
    Paddy Ryan, Terry Walsh, Billy Horrigan, Roy Street,
              Peter Pocock, Bronco McLaughlin
Stunt Double for Doctor Who................Terry Walsh

Production Credits

Production Assistant................................Thea Murray
Assistant Floor Manager ....Linda Graeme
Studio Lighting ....Dennis Channon
Studio Sound ....Colin Dixon
Senior Studio Cameramen....................Peter Granger
                                             & Dave White
Location Lighting............................Dennis Channon
Location Sound ....Hugh Cleverley
Location Film Cameraman ....John Baker
Costume Design ....James Acheson
Make-Up Design ....Jan Harrison
Visual Effects......................................Ian Scoones
Designer...Barry Newbery
Incidental Music ....Dudley Simpson
Director ....Rodney Bennett

Written by Bob Baker & Dave Martin

King Rokon ....Roy Skelton
Zazzka ....Roy Pattison
Abbott ....David Purcell
Doctor Carter.......................................Rex Robinson
Intern..Renu Senta
Professor Watson ....Glyn Houston
Miss Jackson ....Frances Pidgeon
Driscoll...Roy Boyd
Eldrad ....Judith Paris
Kastrian Eldrad....................................Stephen Thorne
Guard..Robin Hargrave
Technic Oban ....Peter Roy
Hospital Nurse.....................................Libbie Ritchie
Computer Voice ....Roy Skelton
Security Guards......Paul Nicholson, Roy Wadsworth,
        Tim Hooper, Robert Lee, Robert Tucker, Michael
                Dewild, Barry Summerford
Men in Radiation Suits ....David Cleeve,
                Keith Simmons
Technicians in Control Room........Rosemary Jollisse,
        Julia Burnett, Kenneth Thomas, Mark Holme,
                Bruce Guest
Path Lab Technicians ....Derek Southern, John Deleiu

Complex Personnel ....Lionel Sansby,
        Douglas Auchterlonie, Roger Salter,
        Margaret Pilleau, Sonia Stratton
Extras..................Michael Wadsworth, David Hyde,
        Colin Jaggard, Carl Edwards, Bob Peters,
        John Tafler, Brian Gear, Bruce Hubble, Alan
        Evans, Simon Jones, Peter Bush, Ken Taylor
Stunt Double for Doctor Carter...........Max Faulkner

Production Credits

Production Assistant....................Marion McDougall
Assistant Floor Manager ....Terry Winders
Studio Lighting ....Derek Slee
Studio Sound ....Brian Hiles
Location Sound.....................................Graham Bedwell
Location Film Cameraman ....Max Samett
Costume Design ....Barbara Lane
Make-Up Design...................................Judy Neame
Visual Effects ....Colin Mapson
Designer...Christine Ruscoe
Incidental Music ....Dudley Simpson
Director ....Lennie Mayne

The Hand of Fear
(Story 4N)
(4 Episodes)

Written by Robert Holmes

Chancellor Goth ....Bernard Horsfall
Castellan Spandrell ....George Pravda
Co-ordinator Engin ....Erik Chitty
The Master ....Peter Pratt
Commander Hildred...........................Derek Seaton
Cardinal Borusa ....Angus Mackay
The President ....Llewellyn Rees
Commentator Runcible ....Hugh Walters
Solis ....Peter Mayock
Gold Usher..Maurice Quick
Voice..Helen Blatch
Tannoy Voice ....Derek Seaton
Time Lord ....Michael Bilton
Camera Technician ....Brian Nolan
Time Lord..John Dawson
Samurai Warrior ....Bernard Horsfall
Soldier in Gas-Mask ....Dave Goody
Train Driver...David Smith
Bi-plane Pilot......................................Chris Jesson
Chancellery Guards........Pat Gorman, Harry Fielder,
                Steve Ismay, Michael Lomax
Time Lords............Willie Bowman, Geoff Witherick,
        George Romanov, Christopher Woods, Reg
        Cranfield, Steve Kelly, Jim Delaney, Sonnie Willis,

Alf Coster, Michael Earl, Richard King, Leslie
Bates, Garth Watkis, Terry Sartain, James Linten,
                Walter Henry, Ronald Mayer
Stunt Double for Doctor Who
& Chancellor Goth ....Terry Walsh
Stund Double for Doctor Who
& The Master.......................................Eddie Powell

Production Credits

Production Assistant ....Nicholas Howard John
Assistant Floor Manager ....Linda Graeme
Studio Lighting ....Brian Clemett
Studio Sound..Clive Gifford
Location Sound.....................................Graham Bedwell
Location Film Cameraman.................Fred Hamilton
Costume Design ....James Acheson & Joan Ellacott
Make-Up Design ....Jean Williams
Visual Effects ....Len Hutton & Peter Day
Designer ....Roger Murray-Leach
Incidental Music ....Dudley Simpson
Director ....David Maloney

The Deadly Assassin
(Story 4P)
(4 Episodes)

The Face of Evil
(Story 4Q)
(4 Episodes)

Written by Chris Boucher

Calib ....Leslie Schofield
Neeva ....David Garfield
Tomas ....Brendan Price
Andor...Victor Lucas
Lugo ....Lloyd McGuire
Sole ....Colin Thomas
Jabel...Leon Eagles
Gentek ....Mike Elles
Acolyte ....Peter Baldock
Guards ....Tom Kelly, Brett Forrest
Xoanon.............................Tom Baker, Rob Edwards,
          Pamela Salem, Roy Herrick, Anthony Frieze
First Assassin ....David Nichol
Second Assassin..................................Harry Fielder
Council Members...........Alan Harris, Michael Reynal
Lugo's Warriors ....Andy Dempsey, Ian Munro,
                                                         John Sarbutt
Tesh in Protective Suit ....Tim Craven
Female Sevateem ....Barbara Bermel
Guards..................................John Bryant, Peter Roy,
                               Paul Barton, Mike Mungarvan
Sevateem ....Peter Deen, Alan Troy, Terry Walsh, Alan
                                                Chuntz, Max Faulkner

Acolytes.............................Tim McCabe, Tom Knox,
                        Ernie Goodyear, David Ludwig,
                          Robert Hastings, Stuart Fell
Sevateem Crowd Voices............Alan Charles Thomas
                          & other members of the cast
Stunt Double for Doctor Who................Terry Walsh
Stuntmen .....Stuart Fell, Alan Chuntz, Max Faulkner

Production Credits

Production Assistant.....................Marion McDougall
Assistant Floor Manager ....Linda Graeme
Studio Lighting ....Derek Slee
Studio Sound ....Colin Dixon
Senior Studio Cameraman ....Colin Reid
Sound (Elstree Shooting) ....Stan Nightingale
Film Cameraman (Elstree Shooting) John McGlashan
Costume Design ....John Bloomfield
Make-Up Design..Ann Ailes
Visual Effects ....Mat Irvine
Designer..Austin Ruddy
Incidental Music ....Dudley Simpson
Director ....Pennant Roberts

The Robots of Death
(Story 4R)
(4 Episodes)

Written by Chris Boucher

Commander Uvanov ....Russell Hunter
Pilot Toos ....Pamela Salem
Chief Fixer Dax/Taren Capel ....David Bailie
Chief Mover Poul ....David Collings
Zilda ....Tania Rogers
Cass ....Tariq Yunus
Mover Borg.....................................Brian Croucher
Chub ....Rob Edwards
Kerril...Peter Sax
SV7 ....Miles Fothergill
D84 ....Gregory de Polnay
Robots:
(V14, V21, V46, D62).............Mark Blackwell Baker
(V6, V32)..Mark Cooper
(V3, V5, V8, V45)............................Richard Seager
(V16, V19, V68) ....John Bleasdale
(D33, D39, D64) ....Peter Langtry
(V2, V4, V9, V17, V28) ....Jeremy Ranchev

Production Credits

Production Assistant.........................Peter Grimwade
Assistant Floor Manager.........................David Tilley
Studio Lighting ....Duncan Brown
Studio Sound...Tony Millier
Film Cameraman (Elstree Shooting) ..Peter Chapman
Costume Design.............................Elizabeth Waller
Make-Up Design..Ann Briggs
Visual Effects ....Richard Conway
Designer..Kenneth Sharp
Incidental Music ....Dudley Simpson
Director ....Michael E. Briant

The Talons of Weng-Chiang
(Story 4S)
(6 Episodes)

Written by Robert Holmes

Henry Gordon Jago ....Christopher Benjamin
Professor Litefoot ....Trevor Baxter
Li H'Sen Chang ....John Bennett
Weng-Chiang/Magnus Greel ....Michael Spice
Mr Sin ....Deep Roy
Casey...Chris Gannon
Sergeant Kyle...David McKail
Police Constable Quick....................Conrad Asquith
Lee ....Tony Then
Buller ....Alan Butler
Ho ....Vincent Wong
Teresa...Judith Lloyd
Coolie...John Wu
Ghoul..Patsy Smart
Cleaner...............................Vaune Craig-Raymond
Singer..Penny Lister
Conductor ....Dudley Simpson
Levitating Girl ....Sally Sinclair
Young Girls............Debbie Cumming, Helen Simnett
Coolies ......Vincent Wong, Arnold, Lee, Dennis Chin
         Sabu Kimura, Fred Leown, Alan Chuntz,
                  Jimmy Ang, Max Faulkner
Extras ....Mary Maxted, James Haswell,
      James Lloyd, Bernard Price, John Cannon,
      Charles Adey Gray, Ronald Musgrove, Kevin
      Sullivan, Lisa Bergmayer, Marie Anthony,
      Tony Randle, Bob Williams, David J.
      Grahame, Bill Hughes, Hentley Young, Chris
      Carrington, Jean Channon, Richard Sheekey

Stunt Double for Doctor Who
& Leela/Giant Rat ....Stuart Fell
Stunt Double for
Weng-Chiang/Magnus Greel ....Max Faulkner
Stunt Doubles for Coolies ....Alan Chuntz,
                                          Max Faulkner

Production Credits

Production Assistant ....Ros Anderson
Assistant Floor Manager ....Linda Graeme
Studio Lighting ....Mike Jeffries
Studio Sound......................................Clive Gifford
Location Lighting.................................John Mason
Location Sound ....Vic Godrich
Location Film Cameraman.................Fred Hamilton
Costume Design ....John Bloomfield
Make-Up Design.............................Heather Stewart
Visual Effects ....Michaeljohn Harris
Designer ....Roger Murray-Leach
Incidental Music ....Dudley Simpson
Director ....David Maloney

Broadcast Dates & Viewing Figures

Note : The figures noted alongside the viewing figures in brackets are the chart positions achieved by the episodes in question.

Season Twelve
(Excluding Robot – Broadcast 28/12/74-18/01/75)

The Ark in Space (Serial 4C) (4 Episodes)
Episode One	25th January 1975	1735-1800hrs
	Running Time – 24'27"	9.4m Viewers (27th)
Episode Two	1st February 1975	1730-1755hrs
	Running Time – 24'49"	13.6m Viewers (5th)
Episode Three	8th February 1975	1730-1755hrs
	Running Time – 24'05"	11.2m Viewers (17th)
Episode Four	15th February 1975	1730-1755hrs
	Running Time – 24'37"	10.2m Viewers (24th)

The Sontaran Experiment (Serial 4B) (2 Episodes)
Episode One	22nd February 1975	1730-1755hrs
	Running Time – 24'27"	11.0m Viewers (18th)
Episode Two	1st March 1975	1730-1755hrs
	Running Time – 25'00"	10.5m Viewers (17th)

Genesis of the Daleks (Serial 4E) (6 Episodes)
Episode One	8th March 1975	1730-1755hrs
	Running Time – 24'30"	10.7m Viewers (23rd)

Episode Two   15th March 1975   1730-1755hrs
                       Running Time – 24'51"   10.5m Viewers (15th)

Episode Three   22nd March 1975   1730-1755hrs
                       Running Time – 22'38"   8.5m Viewers (42nd)

Episode Four   29th March 1975   1730-1755hrs
                       Running Time – 23'38"   8.8m Viewers (36th)

Episode Five   5th April 1975   1730-1755hrs
                       Running Time – 23'27"   9.8m Viewers (30th)

Episode Six   12th April 1975   1755-1820hrs
                       Running Time – 23'30"   9.1m Viewers (26th)

Revenge of the Cybermen

(Serial 4D) (4 Episodes)

Episode One   19th April 1975   1735-1800hrs
                       Running Time – 24'19"   9.5m Viewers (24th)

Episode Two   26th April 1975   1730-1755hrs
                       Running Time – 24'24"   8.3m Viewers (28th)

Episode Three   3rd May 1975   1750-1615hrs
                       Running Time – 24'32"   8.9m Viewers (25th)

Episode Four   10th May 1975   1730-1755hrs
                       Running Time – 23'21"   9.4m Viewers (22nd)

Season Thirteen

Terror of the Zygons (Serial 4F) (4 Episodes)

Episode One   30th August 1975   1745-1810hrs
                       Running Time – 21'41"   8.4m Viewers (29th)

Episode Two   6th September 1975   1745-1810hrs
                       Running Time – 25'08"   6.1m Viewers (61st)

Episode Three   13th September 1975   1745-1810hrs
                       Running Time – 24'09"   8.2m Viewers (32nd)

Episode Four   20th September 1975   1720-1745hrs
                       Running Time – 25'22"   7.2m Viewers (45th)

Planet of Evil (Serial 4H) (4 Episodes)

Episode One   27th September 1975   1745-1810hrs
                       Running Time – 24'02"   10.4m Viewers (19th)

Episode Two   4th October 1975   1745-1810hrs
                   Running Time – 22'30"   9.9m Viewers (24th)

Episode Three   11th October 1975   1805-1830hrs
                   Running Time – 23'50"   9.1m Viewers (29th)

Episode Four   18th October 1975   1745-1810hrs
                   Running Time – 23'43"   10.1m Viewers (26th)

Pyramids of Mars (Serial 4G) (4 Episodes)
Episode One   25th October 1975   1745-1810hrs
                   Running Time – 25'22"   10.2m Viewers (28th)

Episode Two   1st November 1975   1745-1810hrs
                   Running Time – 23'53"   11.3m Viewers (15th)

Episode Three   8th November 1975   1745-1810hrs
                   Running Time – 24'32"   9.4m Viewers (37th)

Episode Four   15th November 1975   1745-1810hrs
                   Running Time – 24'52"   11.7m Viewers (22nd)

The Android Invasion (Serial 4J) (4 Episodes)
Episode One   22nd November 1975   1745-1810hrs
                   Running Time – 24'21"   11.9m Viewers (17th)

Episode Two   29th November 1975   1745-1810hrs
                   Running Time – 24'30"   11.3m Viewers (24th)

Episode Three   6th December 1975   1745-1810hrs
                   Running Time – 24'50"   12.1m Viewers (14th)

Episode Four   13th December 1975   1755-1820hrs
                   Running Time – 24'30"   11.4m Viewers (15th)

The Brain of Morbius (Serial 4K) (4 Episodes)
Episode One   3rd January 1976   1755-1820hrs
                   Running Time – 25'25"   9.5m Viewers (30th)

Episode Two   10th January 1976   1745-1810hrs
                   Running Time – 24'46"   9.3m Viewers (32nd)

Episode Three   17th January 1976   1745-1810hrs
                   Running Time – 25'07"   10.1m Viewers (23rd)

Episode Four   24th January 1976   1755-1820hrs (28th)
                   Running Time – 24'18"   10.2m Viewers

The Seed of Doom (Serial 4L) (6 Episodes)
Episode One   31st January 1976   1800-1825hrs
                   Running Time – 24'10"   11.4m Viewers (16th)

116

Episode Two 7th February 1976 1730-1755hrs
Running Time – 24'09" 11.4m Viewers (30th)

Episode Three 14th February 1976 1755-1820hrs
Running Time – 24'51" 10.3m Viewers (32nd)

Episode Four 21st February 1976 1745-1810hrs
Running Time – 24'26" 11.1m Viewers (23rd)

Episode Five 28th February 1976 1745-1810hrs
Running Time – 25'06" 9.9m Viewers (26th)

Episode Six 6th March 1976 1745-1810hrs
Running Time – 21'51" 11.5m Viewers (15th)

Season Fourteen

The Masque of Mandragora (Serial 4M) (4 Episodes)
Episode One 4th September 1976 1810-1835hrs
Running Time – 24'31" 8.3m Viewers (40th)

Episode Two 11th September 1976 1805-1830hrs
Running Time – 24'44" 9.8m Viewers (22nd)

Episode Three 18th September 1976 1810-1835hrs
Running Time – 24'34" 9.2m Viewers (29th)

Episode Four 25th September 1976 1810-1835hrs
Running Time – 24'45" 10.6m Viewers (23rd)

The Hand of Fear (Serial 4N) (4 Episodes)
Episode One 2nd October 1976 1810-1835hrs
Running Time – 24'50" 10.5m Viewers (24th)

Episode Two 9th October 1976 1750-1815hrs
Running Time – 24'48" 10.2m Viewers (29th)

Episode Three 16th October 1976 1805-1830hrs
Running Time – 24'22" 11.1m Viewers (20th)

Episode Four 23rd October 1976 1800-1825hrs
Running Time – 25'00" 12.0m Viewers (19th)

The Deadly Assassin (Serial 4P) (4 Episodes)
Episode One 30th October 1976 1805-1830hrs
Running Time – 21'13" 11.8m Viewers (15th)

Episode Two 6th November 1976 1805-1830hrs
Running Time – 24'24" 12.1m Viewers (11th)

Episode Three   13th November 1976   1805-1830hrs
Running Time – 24'20"   13.0m Viewers (12th)

Episode Four   20th November 1976   1805-1830hrs
Running Time – 24'30"   11.8m Viewers (12th)

The Face of Evil (Serial 4Q) (4 Episodes)

Episode One   1st January 1977   1820-1845hrs
Running Time – 24'58"   10.7m Viewers (23rd)

Episode Two   8th January 1977   1830-1855hrs
Running Time – 24'58"   11.1m Viewers (19th)

Episode Three   15th January 1977   1820-1845hrs
Running Time – 24'40"   11.3m Viewers (20th)

Episode Four   22nd January 1977   1825-1850hrs
Running Time – 24'46"   11.7m Viewers (19th)

The Robots of Death (Serial 4R) (4 Episodes)

Episode One   29th January 1977   1820-1845hrs
Running Time – 24'06"   12.8m Viewers (14th)

Episode Two   5th February 1977   1820-1845hrs
Running Time – 24'15"   12.4m Viewers (17th)

Episode Three   12th February 1977   1820-1845hrs
Running Time – 23'51"   13.1m Viewers (15th)

Episode Four   19th February 1977   1825-1850hrs
Running Time – 23'42"   12.6m Viewers (18th)

The Talons of Weng Chiang (Serial 4S) (6 Episodes)

Episode One   26th February 1977   1830-1855hrs
Running Time – 24'44"   11.3m Viewers (16th)

Episode Two   5th March 1977   1835-1900hrs
Running Time – 24'26"   9.8m Viewers (28th)

Episode Three   12th March 1977   1830-1855hrs
Running Time – 21'56"   10.2m Viewers (22nd)

Episode Four   19th March 1977   1830-1855hrs
Running Time – 24'30"   11.4m Viewers (21st)

Episode Five   26th March 1977   1830-1855hrs
Running Time – 24'49"   10.1m Viewers (18th)

Episode Six   2nd April 1977   1830-1855hrs
Running Time – 23'26"   9.3m Viewers (32nd)

Repeat Screenings

The Ark in Space
20th August 1975	8.2m Viewers	Edited version for a 70-minute broadcast slot.

Genesis of the Daleks
27th December 1975	7.6m Viewers	Edited version for a 90-minute broadcast slot.
27th July 1982	4.9m Viewers	
2nd August 1982	5.0m Viewers	Edited version for 2x45 minute broadcast slots.
8th January 1993 (1)	2.2m Viewers	
15th January 1993 (2)	2.3m Viewers	
22nd January 1993 (3)	2.3m Viewers	
29th January 1993 (4)	2.1m Viewers	
5th February 1993 (5)	2.2m Viewers	
12th February 1993 (6)	2.3m Viewers	Shown in its original broadcast version.

Planet of Evil
5th July 1976 (1)	5.0m Viewers	
6th July 1976 (2)	5.0m Viewers	
7th July 1976 (3)	4.3m Viewers	
8th July 1976 (4)	3.9m Viewers	Shown in its original broadcast version.

The Sontaran Experiment
9th July 1976	8.2m Viewers	Edited version for a 50-minute broadcast slot.

The Brain of Morbius
4th December 1976	10.9m Viewers	Edited version for a 65-minute broadcast slot.

Pyramids of Mars
27th November 1976	13.7m Viewers	Edited version for a 65-minute broadcast slot.
6th March 1994 (1)	1.1m Viewers	
13th March 1994 (2)	1.1m Viewers	
20th March 1994 (3)	0.8m Viewers	
27th March 1994 (4)	1.0m Viewers	Shown in its original broadcast version.

The Deadly Assassin
4th August 1977 (1)	4.4m Viewers	
11th August 1977 (2)	2.6m Viewers	
18th August 1977 (3)	3.8m Viewers	
25th August 1977 (4)	3.5m Viewers	Shown in its broadcast version, with slight edits for violence.

The Robots of Death
31st December 1977	10.0m Viewers	
1st January 1978	7.0m Viewers	Shown edited into two episodes for 2x50 minute broadcast slots.

Satellite & Video **Superchannel** ran the vast majority of *Doctor Who* stories towards the end of the 1980s, including Hinchcliffe's productions. **UK Gold** completed its second run of stories from 'The Ark in Space' to 'The Talons of Weng-Chiang' by the end of 1995. By January 1996, all of Hinchcliffe's stories, with the two exceptions of 'The Hand of Fear' and 'The Face of Evil', have been made available to purchase on **BBC Video**.

Lost Stories

The Foe From the Future

Written by Robert Banks Stewart

Introduction

'The Foe From the Future' was commissioned by Robert Holmes as a six-part serial in early May 1976, the intention being that it should bring Season Fourteen (and, as it would turn out, the Hinchcliffe era as a whole) to an end.

Robert Banks Stewart never completed more than a draft storyline for the first five episodes because he won a contract as a script editor at Thames Television, which meant that he did not have the time to see the project through to its final draft stage. What follows is the treatment for the first five episodes of the story that was ultimately replaced by 'The Talons of Weng-Chiang'.

Episode One

On the outskirts of a Devon village a small boy pushes a bike with a puncture past the Grange, a grim Gothic mansion just visible over a high wall. As he hurries along in the gathering dusk, the boy looks scared. Owls hoot eerily, the wind moans through the branches. Suddenly, the boy stops as he hears the sound of a horse's hooves, growing louder and louder. Then a ghostly rider, a highwayman, gallops straight through the wall towards him. The boy drops his bike and runs in terror…

In the TARDIS, the Doctor has detected a curious temporal imbalance on Earth. He checks his instruments and tells Leela that something very odd is going on. There's a hitherto unknown twist in the time vortex, and he intends to go and investigate.

The boy has been found in a state of near collapse and taken to the local police constable's house by a vicar, who is a visitor to the district. He tells the constable that the boy was babbling something about a ghostly highwayman. The constable, phoning for the boy's mother to come and collect him, says that most people stay clear of the Grange. Always been ghosts there. Lately, more than usual have been reported, and not so long ago there was the case of the poacher found dead, an expression of terror on his face. The Grange stood empty for many years, but was recently acquired by a mystery buyer, a wealthy recluse who keeps his own small private staff but has never actually been seen by the villagers.

The vicar, intrigued, returns to the Grange late at night, climbing the wall to get in. He is crossing the grounds when he encounters a strange shimmering light and thinks he's about to witness a supernatural event. In fact, it's the TARDIS materialising. As the Doctor and Leela emerge, the vicar is convinced he's seeing ghosts. But the Doctor reassures him that they're nothing of the sort, and says emphatically that there are no such things as ghosts.

In another part of the grounds, at the rear of the Grange, two owls (or other birds) flutter down and sit on an outstretched arm. It's part of a statue, but we don't see any more of it than this at the moment. As the birds land they give a screech and drop dead, as if electrocuted…

The vicar is meanwhile telling the Doctor and Leela about the incident involving the boy and the ghostly highwayman. The vicar says that he's staying at the local inn while taking brass rubbings in the village church. He also tells them about what the police constable has said about the ghosts at the Grange, and the death of the poacher. Never mind ghosts, says the Doctor… there's something else around here that requires investigating.

At the Grange the vicar is getting a stony reception from Storr, the manservant of the owner, Jalnik. No one

APPENDIX THREE: LOST STORIES

can see his master, says the manservant. The vicar notes that everything downstairs is shrouded and dusty. He sees lights flickering on the upstairs floor, but he is firmly turned away.

As the Doctor and Leela move through the grounds, they encounter a ghost themselves: a grim, hooded monk brandishing a dagger ... so much, says Leela, for the Doctor's pronouncement about the non-existence of ghosts! Leela cowers back, scared, but the Doctor grabs a piece of wood and hurls it at the ghostly monk... and the object just passes straight through ...

The vicar is prowling about at the rear of the Grange. He is near the statue when it is enveloped in a blinding bright light. We still don't identify the statue – it is merely a blur in the light, with separate images forming, and a terrible whining noise. The vicar, gradually blinded, stumbles away.

The Doctor and Leela hear a scream. Running to investigate, they find the vicar lying dead in a clearing. He has no injuries and seems to have suffered a heart attack... but his face is a study of terror. Beside him in the dust the Doctor finds a weak attempt to scrawl something. It looks like 'Icarus'. Leaving the body where it is, the Doctor and Leela hurry to the Grange.

They are met by Storr, who explains that his master is unwell and cannot see anybody. The Doctor insists that they must speak to him – there's a dead vicar in the grounds. Then Jalnik's voice cuts in on a relay system from his apartment upstairs. He apologises for not being able to see them in person, but instructs Storr to go with them to the scene.

When they reach the clearing the body of the vicar has disappeared. So has the message in the dust. The manservant consults Jalnik on a walkie-talkie and orders are given to escort the Doctor and Leela from the grounds.

The Doctor and Leela go to the local inn to make enquiries about the vicar. But the landlord says that they must have been seeing ghosts. There's no vicar staying at the inn. Moreover, it would have been impossible for him to be doing brass rubbings in the village church – it's been boarded up and padlocked for twenty years. Just then, the faint sound of a church bell ringing is heard...

Breaking into the church, the Doctor and Leela find the vicar's body dangling from one of the ropes in the belfry, as if he'd hanged himself. They start to get him down when the huge bell overhead breaks loose and comes plunging down towards them...

Episode Two

Reprise. The vicar is being brought down from the bellrope when the bell breaks loose and crashes downwards. The Doctor and Leela manage to jump clear, but the huge bell completely covers the dead vicar.

The local constable arrives on his bike, catching them in the belfry. Obviously someone has tipped him off because he knows that the vicar is dead. The Doctor reckons they'd need a crane to lift the bell, so he stalls for time. What vicar? he asks. Then he suddenly remembers what the vicar wrote in the dust – 'Icarus'. Of course, he says to Leela, I should have realised. The Doctor manages to escape...

The TARDIS has been discovered in the grounds of the Grange. It is being examined outside by Jalnik and Storr. Jalnik's face is covered by a leather mask. He surmises that the TARDIS is some instrument of travel and remarks that they are dealing with no ordinary intruders...

Leela has told the constable that they were at the inn when the bell began to ring. But when the constable, disbelieving her story, takes her to the inn, the place is deserted. So much for her story. The landlord of the place died months ago and it's been closed up. He marches Leela off to his police house to put her in the cell.

Meanwhile, the Doctor is breaking into the grounds of the Grange. He searches about and eludes a couple of zombie-like servants of Jalnik's. Then, at the rear of the Grange, he discovers Icarus – the statue.

We see the Doctor being observed on outside cameras with monitor screens in a laboratory-like control room somewhere in the Grange. A man watching the monitors raises the alarm: intruder in the grounds!

Leela is being put in the single cell attached to the police house. She enquires from the constable about the meaning of the word 'Icarus', and he says that it must refer to the statue in the grounds of the Grange. The house was once owned by Sir Charles Lapney, a famous aviator, and he had the statue erected. The constable locks Leela in and decides that the Doctor has gone to the Grange – and he'll go after him...

At the statue of Icarus, the Doctor witnesses the strange bright light and sees two figures 'emerge' from the statue as human shapes. Ghosts? Unfortunately, he is off guard, watching the event, and he is caught by two of Jalnik's staff.

In a prison room under the Grange the Doctor is questioned by Storr. He is told that he's a meddling nuisance, and that Jalnik will deal with him soon. Storr wants to know where Leela is, but the Doctor won't co-operate. A message comes to say that the village constable has turned up.

The constable explains to Storr that he is looking for the Doctor. He gives away the fact that he is holding Leela in a cell, and says that he has reason to believe that the Doctor has come to the Grange. Storr says that he will keep a look out for him. When the constable has gone, Storr confers with Jalnik, who says the girl must be dealt with immediately. He tells Storr to send someone to the village straight away – one of their number from the Ectoplasmic Suite.

In the cell at the police house Leela hears a scraping sound from outside. We see the constable's dog growling at something, then the dog howls and is dead. A ghostly figure comes through the wall of the cell. Leela screams. At that moment the constable arrives back, unlocks the cell and hurries in. He is killed trying to attack the spectral intruder. Leela escapes.

Leela gets to the Grange and scouts about. She overhears one of Jalnik's men talking about the Doctor in the prison room, and finds a way to the underground complex. She lays out a guard and rescues the Doctor.

Jalnik finishes supervising some work in the laboratory and decides to question the Doctor. He discovers that the Doctor has escaped, and then hears that Leela also got away. He is furious. Their whole operation is at risk. Search for them both, and if necessary, kill!

Leela is all for getting as far away from the Grange as possible, but the Doctor is determined to find out what's going on. He has already decided that the people they are dealing with are from the future – not ghosts from the past. They discover a machine used for projecting ghosts – obviously used to scare people away. There is a wide variety of traditional ghosts – nuns, highwaymen, cavaliers, the monk, etc. – and the Doctor playfully starts projecting some of the figures, causing some confusion in the grounds among Jalnik's staff. As a result, the Doctor and Leela are recaptured.

Jalnik has the Doctor and Leela brought before him before they are disposed of. Somehow, the Doctor succeeds in pulling off Jalnik's leather mask, exposing a face that is a human travesty...

Episode Three

Reprise. The Doctor rips the mask from Jalnik's face to expose his horrible, mutated features. Jalnik wants to know: Who are you, Doctor? The Doctor explains about his discovery of the twist in the time vortex and his realisation that Jalnik and the others are from the future. Jalnik says it's true. He was the first, and something went wrong with the molecular transfer in his case, hence the malformation of his face. He is boss of the spearhead. Soon they will remove all existing humans from the Earth, and the people of the future will flow back into the present. Why? ask the Doctor. Sorry, says Jalnik, I can't tell you any more. You will have to face my superiors, the Council of Twelve... 4,000 AD... and Jalnik cannot guarantee the efficiency of the time machine on the reverse journey...

The Doctor and Leela are put into a time machine, and they go into a trance-like state. Then they twitch and groan in some unconscious agony, finally disintegrate and disappear...

A large white transference dome – the other end of the time tunnel. The Doctor comes round and finds Leela beside him, apparently dead. Then he discovers that she is simply a hollow shell: all her organs got left behind. The Doctor pleads with a guard for something to be done before it's too late. But the guard says he must wait for the supervisor. The Doctor clubs him and busies himself with the controls, changing the settings, etc. It works: Leela is whole again and they escape into...

... the training section of a future world complex. It's night, and the place is deserted. They find replicas of the past – 20th Century pubs, offices... objects... all museum pieces. There are instruction boards (or prompter panels) with lessons on what to do in the 20th Century.

The supervisor comes to the transference dome with one of the leading members of the Council of Twelve, Kostal, who is eager to question the Doctor. They find the unconscious guard... Yes, says Kostal, they were very violent in the 20th Century. The alarm is raised. Find the Doctor and the girl!

The Doctor and Leela hear the alarm being raised. It is daytime by now, and the training programme is about to start. Their best cover is to join the trainees. The people undergoing the course wear various styles of 20th Century dress... some of them with glaring mistakes in matching their clothes: boiler suit with an umbrella and bowler hat. The Doctor and Leela join separate groups and are accepted as trainees.

The guard is brought to try and identify the Doctor and Leela, but they switch their garb and get away with it. Nevertheless, the Doctor is too free with advice for his own good, correcting mistakes, showing people how to use certain artefacts like old fashioned telephones in the proper manner. He arouses suspicion. And all the time he is trying to find out why these people want to go backwards in time. Surely, says one man called Osin, everyone knows about the Pantophagen? He is especially suspicious of the Doctor, and when he talks to another trainee, Leela overhears. Osin leaves the group and she follows him.

Leela shadows Osin to the main control complex, where he wants to see Kostal, the Council 'Hawk'. She lays him out before he can make his report. As she hurries to get back and warn the Doctor there is an alert call, and on the television screens she sees…

The Pantophagen – two giant, locust-like creatures who arrive like airships and begin to attack, devouring everything in their path, munching up a whole town (model) voraciously.

Leela gets to the training area and tells the Doctor about what she's seen, and also that it's only a matter of time before Osin recovers and informs Kostal and the rest of the Council of Twelve where they are. The Doctor and Leela make themselves scarce…

Osin duly reports to Kostal, who is about to attend a Council session. We hear about the threat of the Pantophagen… how they have returned… the hope that they will take off again and find some other part of Europe or beyond to munch.

The Doctor and Leela, meanwhile, go looking for the Pantophagen. They come upon them, munching everything in their path, and Leela falls in front of one of them. It hovers over her…

Episode Four

Reprise. The Doctor and Leela are threatened by the Pantophagen. The Doctor manages to drag Leela clear, but they see homes and people being eaten by the giant locusts.

Running from the scene, the Doctor and Leela are picked up by a man driving a futuristic vehicle. His name is Shibac. He thinks they belong to his age, but they explain to him that they are intruders from the 20th Century. They are stopped by guards searching for them, but Shibac doesn't turn them in…

Kostal hears about the latest escape of the Doctor and Leela. He is in touch with Jalnik in the past (by a video link?) and learns more about them in the 20th Century and of the Doctor's powers. We realise that Jalnik and Kostal are partners in the scheme to transfer the people of the future to the past, but they intend to rule together when the switch is complete.

Meanwhile, Shibac has hidden the Doctor and Leela, and he explains what it's all about. The two giant locusts, the Pantophagen, have been flying about and steadily eating up great tracts of the Earth. They move about at will and nothing, it seems, can stop them. The Council of Twelve have hit upon the idea of returning everybody in time, for a fresh start. Shibac, like many others, doesn't agree with this policy, but Jalnik and Kostal swayed the Council, and Jalnik wanted to be the first explorer back in time.

Kostal talks with Osin about the search for the Doctor and Leela. He promises Osin status if they are captured.

Shibac returns to the hiding place to report to the Doctor that he has found a member of the Council to talk to. The Doctor believes that he might be able to give the Council some advice about how to set about ridding the world of Pantophagen, but Osin has been tracking Shibac, and when the Doctor leaves to talk to the moderate member of the Council he is caught and taken off secretly to be imprisoned by Kostal.

But Leela gives everyone the slip. The Pantophagen have attacked again, and she had to get past them to reach the moderate Council man, Geflo…

In the laboratory at the Grange, Jalnik checks on the progress of the device for destroying current humans. Completion of it is not far away, but he is impatient to use it and irked when told to wait for the Council's final go-ahead. He tells Storr, however, that he intends to use the time transference machine to go and talk to his ally, Kostal, and argue for the immediate implementation of his plan.

Leela has managed to reach Geflo, the Council member who is Shibac's friend. She explains to him that the Doctor is no enemy, and that he may be able to help with their problem over the Pantophagen, but he is being held by Kostal. Geflo promises to try and secure his release.

In the transference dome, Jalnik materialises, but is forced to go on wearing his leather mask – his face cannot be re-transformed in the future. Kostal greets him and tells him about the Doctor's escape and recapture.

The Pantophagen are still ravaging the landscape.

As she returns to the hiding place, Leela is spotted by Osin and caught.

Meanwhile, Jalnik comes to the Doctor's prison to gloat over him. He makes it quite clear that he will go ahead and destroy humanity in the 20th Century, whether the Council of Twelve agrees or not.

Leela is horrified when Jalnik arrives in his mask, his head showing through the door's observation panel. He asks the guard to unlock the cell as he intends to kill her. But when he comes in and removes his mask... it's the Doctor!

The Doctor and Leela escape from the complex. He wants another look at the Pantophagen. They steal a vehicle and drive out to observe the giant locusts. Unfortunately, Osin is hidden in the vehicle, and he has orders from Kostal to kill them. He is staking them out when the Pantophagen suddenly attack...

Episode Five

Reprise. Osin prepares the Doctor and Leela for death by the Pantophagen, when they suddenly attack. The Doctor manages to free himself and Leela, and they grab the vehicle and escape. Osin is eaten by one of the locusts.

Kostal orders Jalnik to return to his outpost in the 20th Century. His face, in any case, is not a very good advertisement for his transference.

The Doctor and Leela go to see Geflo, and the Doctor discusses their efforts to fight the Pantophagen menace. He hears that the world no longer had any weaponry to deal with such threats.

The Doctor is brought before the Council and has a showdown with them. He argues against their morality in wanting to take over the past. Alright, they say, show us what you can do, Doctor...

From the various 20th Century artefacts the Doctor constructs some kind of gun. He goes out to deal with the Pantophagen, but his weapon fails...

The Council hear that Jalnik has sabotaged the time transference machine, and that he intends to go it alone in the 20th Century. Kostal is revealed as his ally, who intends to join him, but has been double-crossed. Kostal pays the penalty by being thrown out to the locusts.

The Doctor succeeds in repairing the time-transference machinery, only he isn't sure if it's going to work alright. He and Leela might end up like Jalnik, but they must try and get back to the 20th Century and stop him.

They enter the time machine. Is it working? We find them materialising at the other end... They are alright. Unfortunately, the Pantophagen are drawn through the time process as well, and now pose a threat to the 20th Century!

Note And that's as far as Banks Stewart got. The only element that transferred into 'The Talons of Weng-Chiang' was the fact that the villain wore a leather mask, with his disfigurements having come from a malfunctioning time machine as well. The episode ending for part two also survived in Robert Holmes's story.

The story is structured in the way that Holmes had devised for the latter six-parters of his years with Hinchcliffe, with the first two episodes being a seemingly self-contained story, which suddenly changes directions and carries the plot thread through into what is effectively a new scenario entirely. This had been done with 'The Seeds of Doom', and it's obviously what Banks Stewart planned to do with 'The Foe from the Future'.

The Lost Valley

Written by Philip Hinchcliffe

Introduction

In November 1978 Philip Hinchcliffe submitted a story outline to Graham Williams and his then script editor, Douglas Adams, for them to consider as a potential serial for Season Seventeen. On January 3rd 1979, Hinchcliffe, who was still at the BBC, received this reply from Adams.

'Thanks for letting us read this storyline. Now that Graham and I have had a chat about it, these are our feelings. First, we are convinced that it will be over-expensive. I know you don't agree, but this may be because in real terms the show's budget is lower than it was three or four years ago.

'More importantly, there are wide areas of conflict with other stories we have in the pipeline. The use of an anachronistic Earth setting conflicts with John Lloyd's story, we are already heavily into time freezes and time loops with Baker-Martin and with Alistair Beaten, David Fisher's script is all about a stranded alien waiting for the arrival of a spacefleet and concludes with the Doctor de-activating a dangerous sun.

'I think these factors taken mean we won't be able to use this storyline, but many thanks for letting us see it… Douglas Adams.'

The following text is the storyline itself, reproduced exactly as Hinchcliffe sent it in.

Premise

This is a story about an invasion of Earth. The invaders – The Lurons – are an intelligent humanoidal race with super-efficient bodies. Consequently, they live a much longer time scale than Earthlings. A century can seem like an hour to them.

They are resourceful and determined. They have journeyed light years across galaxies in their giant spaceship and have selected Earth for colonisation. Their aim (they say) is to live with humans in peaceful co-existence, but could Mother-Earth ever be the same again? Their real motive is to enslave mankind and make us subservient to their superior technology.

Lurons are yellow skinned and yellow eyed, with elongated heads and funny ears. In the right clothes, dark glasses and bad lighting, they can pass for humans.

They are extremely methodical and very cautious. In 1870 (our time) their giant spaceship arrived undetected in our solar system. They then despatched an emissary to Earth in a small scout ship. Unfortunately, it was damaged by meteorites, and the emissary (GODRIN) and his craft crashlanded in the South American jungle (instead of a field near London).

Background

Having lost contact with his mothership and unable to repair his craft, GODRIN is temporarily marooned. The waiting Lurons don't know what's happened to their emissary, but being cautious types, they will do nothing for a while (in Earth time this means a few decades, if not centuries).

Now, Lurons carry their own time scale with them like a giant magnetic field (more of this later), and so the time field of GODRIN's scout ship extends over a largish area, keeping everything in and around it in 1870, so to speak.

Nor is the jungle entirely deserted. The ancient and mythical city of Maygor (the fabled 'city of gold') lies hidden and buried not a million miles from GODRIN's crashed ship. Barbaric natives – descendants of the once great civilisation of Maygor – inhabit this region. They retain a few secrets and rites of their forbears, including a huge carved mask representing their oracular Godhead, and from which in the olden days their 'God' spoke. They also know where the gold is hidden.

GODRIN quickly susses all this and assumes a God-like position in their midst. (This entails getting behind the mask and 'speaking' to the tribe, thereby animating their ancient God with his yellow eyes and conveniently fulfilling some old prediction). However, all this is no use in mending his scout ship.

At the same time, a rapacious and cunning English explorer has set out (in 1870) on a perilous mission to discover the mythical Maygors and their mythical hidden gold. He arrives in the jungle a couple of years after

GODRIN has crashed, and amongst other things, he comes across a strange skull which (the DOCTOR will later surmise) belongs to GODRIN's pilot, who was killed in the crash and given a shallow burial.

Last piece of background: since the advent of air travel, part of the South American continent has become renowned for its 'Bermuda Triangle' effect. Over the years, various aircraft – civil and military – have disappeared in the jungle, adding spice to its mystery. They have, in fact, simply flown into GODRIN's time-bubble. Sometimes the planes reappeared and continued their flight. Usually, they mysteriously lost control and crashlanded, never to be heard of again.

Story Proper

The story opens with the DOCTOR paying good old London a visit. He shows ROMANA the sights and she enjoys being 'The Tourist'. He also looks up some old friends (whomever we like) and he is persuaded by one to give a talk on the lesser known Brazilian ragwort (or whatever). The DOCTOR good-naturedly agrees, only to find the lecture is to take place in South America! Amused for once by the notion of old-fashioned transportation, the DOCTOR duly flies out with ROMANA. (Being thoughtful, he also bones up on where he's going – for the DOCTOR, a matter of a few minutes in the British Museum).

In flight, the aircraft starts behaving oddly, and after a flightdeck drama, crashlands deep in the Brazilian jungle. All radio equipment is destroyed. The DOCTOR sees to the survivors, then leaves ROMANA in charge and sets off for help. While this is going on, we see 'eyes' watching from the jungle.

After suitable excitements, the DOCTOR is captured by a group of natives. He is taken to a camp where he meets a Victorian explorer.

'Professor Perkins? But, you were lost in the Brazilian jungle in 1873!' exclaims the DOCTOR, displaying his phenomenal knowledge of *The Times* back numbers. The DOCTOR has indeed been captured by the Professor's scouts. The PROF. explains something of his expedition (omitting all mention of gold) and grows deeply suspicious of the DOCTOR, who seems to know more than he should. He decides to keep the DOCTOR captive. The DOCTOR realises that someone is meddling with time!

Back at the aircraft, ROMANA and Co. are attacked with blow darts by a different set of natives – wild, farouche, frightening. They are captured and led away.

From talking to the native bearers, the DOCTOR learns of the city of gold and of other unspeakables, including a strange skull that the PROF. has in his possession. The expedition comes across a large rusting wreckage. Only the DOCTOR realises that it's an aircraft.

ROMANA and Co. are taken to a part of the hidden city. ROMANA notices some artefact from the Luron scout ship which is not 'of Earth'. Her captors talk about submitting her to the judgement of their God. She is led before the giant facemask. It speaks in a terrifying voice and she sees the 'yellow eyes'. They are clearly alien!

Remainder of the Plot in Brief:

The alien (GODRIN) realises that ROMANA is 'different' from the others. He is told of the crashed aircraft from the sky and begins to see a means of accomplishing his mission and reaching civilisation (i.e. London).

The PROF. is determined at all costs to get his hands on the Maygor gold, even if it means murdering the DOCTOR. First, however, he will use the DOCTOR's cleverness to find the city. This happens and some kind of deal takes place between GODRIN and the mercenary PROF., whereby the PROF. gets the gold and GODRIN has the dangerous DOCTOR delivered into his hands.

Alongside this will be some subplot, involving ROMANA and unspeakable ancient Maygor rites, which the DOCTOR has to deal with en route.

The DOCTOR and GODRIN finally confront one another (by which time, GODRIN will have revealed his ruthless determination to the audience by finally disposing of the PROF.), and all is suspiciously 'sweetness and light'. The DOCTOR realises that GODRIN is a risk to Earth, but is not sure how. As yet, he has no proof of other Lurons, because GODRIN plays things close to his chest. GODRIN tells the DOCTOR that all he wants is a lift to London. With the help of booster equipment from GODRIN's scout craft, they will be able to repair and 'jump start' such a simple piece of machinery as an Earthling airliner.

This they do. The DOCTOR is worried. Why does GODRIN wish to go to London? (Because it was the centre of the civilised world in 1870). Is GODRIN the only Luron? (No, millions of them are lurking on the edge of the solar system, just waiting for GODRIN to give the all clear.)

Back in 1979, the lost jet miraculously reappears in British airspace and radio contact is restored. The DOCTOR mentions their strange extra passenger. The jet touches down, and GODRIN cleverly slips off the plane. Via Jodrell Bank or some other fiendish means, he signals his mates to come on down. This they do, entering Earth's time zone for the first time (so, we're back in 1870).

The gigantic Luron spaceship (a mile long) appears in the heavens and terrifies the world. It hovers over Windsor Great Park and blots out the sun. A ferry ship is sent down. Statesmen and Chiefs of Staff are ordered aboard for parley. All seems friendly. The Lurons explain how they were forced to leave their home planet because of destructive solar winds, and how all they want is a compatible planet on which to live in peaceful harmony.

The statesmen and military return to earth. While on board, one of them has secretly been 'doctored' (or maybe 'doubled') and he now quietly starts ordering the defence air forces to stand down. Also, despite a promise to the contrary, Luron ferry ships land contingents of Luron infiltrators in London, and they start to take over key positions (carefully hiding their ears).

The DOCTOR is not idle during all of this. He twigs to the Lurons' game, and by trickery, he and ROMANA gain access to the Luron mothership. There they dismantle a Very Important Piece of Equipment at the heart of the great vessel. This is the Luron equivalent of an atomic sub's nuclear reactor, the source not only of all electrical power, but also of the Luron 'Lifeforce'. It is the Luron's 'Sun' in miniature, which they have simulated and brought with them and without which they will all die. Their mothership will always hover in Earth's sky, because to remove it would be to destroy their Luron habitat (including their own time-field). Leave it in the sky, however, and these same solar rays (so close) will destroy mankind in a matter of months.

Singlehandedly, the DOCTOR deals with this peril, risking his own life, as he penetrates to the very core of the artificial Sun. He solves the problem thus: either he blows up the ship and all the Lurons die (a bit strong); or he incapacitates the 'Sun' for a while, some die, and the rest agree to leave Earth in peace and find another planet. The action denouement is the DOCTOR, still trapped on the Luron mothership until the very last minute.

Of course, he escapes... or, does he? Depending on the next adventure or Tom's contract!...

Note: On the final page of the treatment, there's a hand-written note in pencil from Douglas Adams, which simply reads – 'Close Encounters Of The Expensive Kind?'...

From:

Room No. &
Building:

Douglas Adams, Script Editor 'Doctor Who'

505 Union Ho   Tel.
                Ext.: 4109   date: 3rd January, 1979

DOCTOR WHO AND 'THE LOST VALLEY'

Subject:

Philip Hinchliffe

To:

Thanks for letting us read this storyline.
Now that Graham and I have had a chat about
it, these are our feelings.

First, we are convinced that it will be
over expensive.   I know you don't agree,
but this may be because in real terms the
show's budget is lower than it was three
or four years ago.

More importantly, there are wide areas of
conflict with other stories we have in the
pipeline.   The use of an anachronistic
Earth setting conflicts with John Lloyd's
story, we are already heavily into time
freezes and time loops with Baker-Martin
and with Alistair Beaton, David Fisher's
script is all about a stranded alien
waiting for the arrival of a spacefleet
and concludes with the Doctor de-activating
a dangerous sun.

I think these factors taken together mean
we won't be able to use this storyline,
but many thanks for letting us see it.

(Douglas Adams)

Enc: storyline
jj